CYBER WAR: DEFINITIONS, DETERRENCE, AND FOREIGN POLICY

HEARING

BEFORE THE

COMMITTEE ON FOREIGN AFFAIRS
HOUSE OF REPRESENTATIVES

ONE HUNDRED FOURTEENTH CONGRESS

FIRST SESSION

SEPTEMBER 30, 2015

Serial No. 114–106

Printed for the use of the Committee on Foreign Affairs

Available via the World Wide Web: http://www.foreignaffairs.house.gov/ or
http://www.gpo.gov/fdsys/

U.S. GOVERNMENT PUBLISHING OFFICE

96–817PDF WASHINGTON : 2015

For sale by the Superintendent of Documents, U.S. Government Publishing Office
Internet: bookstore.gpo.gov Phone: toll free (866) 512–1800; DC area (202) 512–1800
Fax: (202) 512–2104 Mail: Stop IDCC, Washington, DC 20402–0001

CONTENTS

CYBER WAR: DEFINITIONS, DETERRENCE, AND FOREIGN POLICY

WEDNESDAY, SEPTEMBER 30, 2015

House of Representatives,
Committee on Foreign Affairs,
Washington, DC.

The committee met, pursuant to notice, at 10:14 a.m. in room 2172, Rayburn House Office Building, Hon. Ed Royce (chairman of the committee) presiding.

Mr. SALMON [presiding]. This hearing will come to order. This morning we will consider the growing threats to U.S. national security in cyberspace. It is no exaggeration to say that we are at the dawn of a new age of warfare. Computers and the Internet have connected people around the world. However, reliance on these technologies has also made us vulnerable to cyber attacks from other countries, terrorists, and criminals.

So much so that the Pentagon now counts cyberspace as the fifth domain of warfare alongside land, air, sea, and space. Whether or not an all-out cyber war occurs, it is clear that we are in a state of ongoing cyber conflict. The White House, the State Department, and the Department of Defense have all been hacked, and, of course, the Office of Personnel Management had the sensitive information of more than 21 million Americans compromised.

In the private sector, hackers have crashed the computers of Sony executives, seized the personal information of more than 78 million people from the Nation's second largest health insurer, and stolen the credit and debit card information of more than 40 million customers of a major retailer. The magnitude of this theft is staggering, yet it is said that it takes companies an average of 205 days to even realize their system has been breached.

Across the globe, Estonia found itself at the opposite end of a crippling Russia-backed denial of service attack. A computer worm shut down the air force and navies of France and Great Britain for a time. And an attack by North Korea, coined Dark Seoul, crippled South Korea's banking system.

In the coming years, it is likely that Iran will pour more resources into cyber weapons. These have already been used against the U.S. Navy, American banks, a Las Vegas casino, and Saudi Arabia's largest oil producer, all without setting off significant retaliation. Indeed, it has been said that it is exactly the lack of international norms in responding that make cyber weapons so attractive to Russia, China, Iran, and North Korea. So we have a lot of work to do.

Our top intelligence officer told Congress earlier this month that the U.S. lacks both the substance and the mind-set to deterrence. Indeed, last spring the President issued an Executive order that would allow him to target individuals or organizations deemed responsible for computer attacks, but this new order, similar to the way in which terrorists of nuclear proliferators are targeted, has yet to be used. So the President's recent comment that offense is moving faster than defense is putting it mildly.

From the private sector to government, our country is taking body blow after body blow in cyberspace. Why aren't we hitting back? As one observer notes, we have a deterrence deficit.

The new agreement between the United States and China on economic espionage would be a step forward if China actually abides by it. And others, like Iran and Russia, will be watching closely how the United States responds to what is perhaps the greatest theft in history.

We look forward to hearing from our witnesses, what is cyber war and how does it differ from cyber conflict and cyber espionage? Could better attribution techniques be developed to help the United States deter cyberattacks? What is the role of diplomacy in containing cyber conflict? Do the international norms surrounding traditional warfare apply? And what are the foreign policy implications of continued cyber infiltrations and espionage?

We look forward to our witnesses' testimony as we consider U.S. responses to one of the most urgent problems facing the United States.

And I now turn to the ranking member for any opening comments he might have.

Mr. ENGEL. Well, thank you very much, Mr. Salmon. And to our witnesses, welcome to the Foreign Affairs Committee. We badly need your expertise, because our focus today is a new frontier when it comes to enhancing American security, and I agree with everything that my colleague just said.

For years, cyber attacks from overseas have posed a growing threat to the United States. Cybercrimes, such as a breach of the credit card systems at Target stores by Russian hackers in 2013, have put millions of American consumers at risk. Cyber espionage by foreign governments, the recent attack on the Office of Personnel Management, for example, threatens to expose national security information and violates the privacy of many, many American citizens.

Today this committee is focusing on cyber war. That is a relatively new term and we still don't have a consensus about what it generally means, exactly means. Generally speaking, cyber war is understood as something different from the attacks that the United States has already experienced.

So today I hope we can provide a little clarity on what we mean by cyber war. When does an act of espionage or vandalism cross the line and become an act of war? What would it take for a cyber attack to violate prohibitions against the use of force under the Laws of Armed Conflict? And regardless of the terminology we use, what should we be doing to protect the security of the United States and our citizens?

I think it is urgent that we move quickly to address this challenge, because it is unlike any threat we have seen in the past. In recent history, the power of our military and safety of our shores have kept the violence of conventional warfare at a distance for most Americans, but technology has made the world smaller and more interconnected, for better and for worse.

A conventional war today could easily be accomplished by cyber attacks on critical infrastructure here at home. Our power grid, air traffic control systems, water treatment facilities, or freight infrastructure could all be targeted.

Our private sector is also a likely target. The Governments of China, Russia, Iran and other nations understand the value of American business secrets and intellectual property. That is why the Justice Department indicted five members of the Chinese military conspiring to steal American trade secrets in the metal and energy sectors and pass them along to Chinese businesses. I hope our witnesses can provide some insight about the best ways to shore up our defenses against these threats.

And as we guard against this danger at home, I think America has a role to play around the world helping to establish standards for this cyber activity, bringing governments together to prevent and put a stop to cyber conflict. We led the way when it came to conventional conflict, we can lead the way again. In fact, we have already taken positive steps.

In 2011, the Obama administration released an international strategy for cyberspace, calling for stronger diplomacy in private-public partnership to deal with this issue. A year later, we pushed to classify cyber activities causing death, injury, or significant destruction as a use of force under international law. We worked with Russia and China through the U.N. to limit the threat of cyberattacks against critical infrastructure. And we took another big step last week.

Before Chinese President Xi visited the United States, several members of this committee wrote to President Obama, singling out the Chinese Government's cyber theft of intellectual property as a major concern. So I was very pleased that on Friday, the administration announced a huge win for U.S. companies. President Obama secured a commitment from the Chinese Government to stop engaging in state-sponsored cyber theft of intellectual property, including trade secrets and confidential business information.

What is more, the Chinese agreed to work with us to prosecute cyber criminals targeting American assets. This is a significant achievement, but, of course, we need to make sure that China holds up its end of the deal. Talk is cheap. We have to make sure they produce, and we have to produce by being tough.

Mr. Chairman, let me just add, even though it is off topic, last week in, my opinion, we achieved another landmark in U.S.-China cooperation on another critical threat, climate change. After years of pressure from the U.S. at very high levels, the Chinese will start a cap and trade system to curb carbon emissions in their country. I believe it is a very important step.

Let me close by saying that while we have taken steps at home and shown leadership around the world, we still have a long way to go just to understand the nature and threat of cyber war, let alone what is necessary to contain this threat and protect our interests.

So, again, let me thank our witnesses. I look forward to a good discussion and look forward to hearing their expertise. Thank you, Mr. Chairman.

Mr. SALMON. Thank you.

This morning we are pleased to be joined by a distinguished panel. First, Dr. James Lewis is a Senior Fellow and Director in the Strategic Technologies Program at the Center for Strategic and International Studies. Before joining CSIS, Dr. Lewis served in both the Department of State and the Department of Commerce. Welcome.

Dr. Catherine Lotrionte. Is that correct?

Ms. LOTRIONTE. Yes.

Mr. SALMON. Is the Director of the Institute for Law, Science and Global Security at Georgetown University, where she teaches courses on national security law, U.S. intelligence law, and international law. Welcome.

Mr. Bob Butler is an Adjunct Senior Fellow in the Technology and National Security Program at the Center for New American Security. Mr. Butler has led a long career in information technology, intelligence, and national security in both the private and public sector. And he is going to the best State in the country this afternoon, Arizona. So happy to have that.

Without objection, the witnesses' full prepared statements will be made part of the record, and members will have 5 calendar days to submit statements, questions, and extraneous materials for the record.

Dr. Lewis, would you please summarize your remarks.

STATEMENT OF JAMES ANDREW LEWIS, PH.D., SENIOR FEL-LOW AND DIRECTOR, STRATEGIC TECHNOLOGIES PRO-GRAM, CENTER FOR STRATEGIC AND INTERNATIONAL STUDIES

Mr. LEWIS. Thank you, Mr. Chairman, and thanks to the committee for inviting me to testify.

Cybersecurity is a foreign policy problem, so it falls squarely in the jurisdiction of this committee. While much of our discussion focuses on domestic solutions, these by themselves are inadequate to secure our networks against foreign opponents. Five countries have advanced cyber attack capabilities: The U.S., the U.K., Russia, China, and Israel. And several other countries are developing these capabilities. They include Iran and North Korea, both of which who have used cyber attacks against American companies.

So far when we look at these countries, they use their cyber attack capabilities in a manner that is consistent with their national military strategies and their policies. This means that cyber war is unlikely outside of some larger conflict. If that conflict were to occur, however, whether it was over the South China Sea or over the Russian interventions around the world, our opponents would use cyber attack to disrupt command and control systems and the software that controls advanced weapons. Both Russia and China have probed the most advanced U.S. weapons systems to prepare for this.

Critical infrastructure is a second order target. Countries will attack it when they think they control the risk of escalation or when they are desperate, but it is vulnerable and it is a target that both Russia and China have probed.

While there is agreement that international law, including the Laws of Armed Conflict, apply to cyber war, there remains areas of significant dispute, particularly over what qualifies as an armed attack or use of force in cyberspace. There is a gray area since a cyber attack can cause disruption without causing destruction or casualties. We have seen this with Iran's attack on Saudi Aramco and North Korea's action against Sony. How the Laws of Armed Conflict apply to this gray area is unclear.

The concepts of use and force in armed attack underpin our treaty obligations for mutual defense. The U.S. has worked with its allies in NATO and in Asia to modify our existing treaties to ensure that the use of force in cyberspace is covered by them, is part of mutual defense.

The definition of armed attack and use of force also determine deterrence thresholds. And I noted that, I think, the chairman talked about a deterrence deficit. We clearly have that. It is a major problem.

In response to Sony and to Iran's actions against the Sands casino, the administration took steps to strengthen deterrence, including public discussion of our improved attribution capabilities and the creation of new cybersecurity sanctions. The goal was to create a credible threat.

It is too early to tell if this has worked, but traditional military espionage does not work and will not work against cyber crime or cyber espionage. The U.S. needs to find something other than military threats to stop these activities. Indictments and sanctions can threaten deterrence, but more work is needed, and this is where the committee can play an important role.

It could consider, among other things, expanded oversight of diplomatic activities, including the implementation and compliance with alliance commitments and bilateral agreements, such as the recent agreement with China, and the work in the U.N. to build norms on responsible state behavior. It could look at legislative actions to strengthen countermeasures.

We won't always go to war over cyber espionage, in fact, we are unlikely to ever go to war over cyber espionage, but there are countermeasures such as sanctions or other penalties that we know have an effect on our opponents. It would be useful to provide greater clarity into the legal basis for the authorization of the use of force in cyberspace.

Finally, you mentioned the existing 2011 International Strategy. This needs to be revised. It was written for a much different security environment, and it needs a second look, something that either this administration or the next will have to do. Cybersecurity poses a difficult challenge for foreign policy. Congress can help by providing oversight and guidance on its international and diplomatic aspects.

I thank the committee for the opportunity to testify, and will be happy to answer any questions.

Mr. SALMON. Thank you.

[The prepared statement of Mr. Lewis follows:]

CSIS | CENTER FOR STRATEGIC & INTERNATIONAL STUDIES

Statement before the
House Committee on Foreign Affairs

"CYBER WAR: DEFINITIONS, DETERRENCE AND FOREIGN POLICY"

A Statement by:

James A. Lewis

Director and Senior Fellow Strategic Technologies Program

Center for Strategic and International Studies (CSIS)

September 30, 2015

2172 Rayburn House Office Building

WWW.CSIS.ORG   1616 RHODE ISLAND AVENUE NW   TEL. (202) 887-0200
WASHINGTON, D.C 20036   FAX (202) 775.3199

I would like to thanks the Committee for this opportunity to testify. Cybersecurity is a central issue in American foreign policy, on a par with terrorism or proliferation. There can be no cybersecurity without international agreement on state behavior. The internet provides countries with new ways to grow and trade, but it is also a means of coercion, espionage, crime, and attack. The ability conduct remote exploits on computer networks (known colloquially as "hacking") has become another tool for state's to use against each other.

While much of the discussion of cybersecurity has focused on things like information sharing, critical infrastructure protection, or incentives for private action, these concepts are largely defensive, reactive and ineffective. They would harden American networks to some degree, but not enough to improve the situation. Building a better Maginot line is not good strategy. We face determined and well resourced foreign opponents who are responsible for the most damaging malicious cyber actions against the U.S. This makes cybersecurity a foreign policy problem. It is not technical; it is political and requires diplomatic and military responses.

We can assess the cybersecurity problem by looking at the numbers. There have been thousands of incidents of cyber espionage and cybercrime (the most expensive usually victimize financial institutions). In contrast, there have been perhaps a dozen incidents of countries using cyber tools for political coercion, and only three or four incidents that would qualify as the use of force or armed attack. Reaching international agreement on what qualifies as the use of force or an armed attack is a crucial problem for international negotiation and agreement on cybersecurity, and continued ambiguity hampers the application of international law and limits our ability to deter cyber attacks.

Another set of numbers is also telling. Two countries, Russia and China, are responsible for most of the malicious cyber actions taken against the United States, Chinese actors, usually from the People Liberation Army, are responsible for more than half of all economic espionage in the United States, more than all other countries in the world put together. Russian criminal groups, operating with the approval of the Russian government, are responsible for most of the major cybercrimes against U.S. financial institutions. If these two counties behaved responsibly and cooperated in law enforcement, the magnitude of the cyber problem would diminish appreciably.

A unilateral approach to cybersecurity will not work. The U.S. ultimately needs to persuade or compel those nations who take action against us in cyberspace to stop. A purely defensive strategy will not work. Nor can we deter cyber espionage and crime. This means that negotiations, with allies, opponents, and the undecided nations, are indispensable for improving cybersecurity. These negotiations will be difficult and slow, but they are essential and this makes cybersecurity a topic that should be of central concern to this committee.

What does "cyber war" look like?

Cyberwar has been a topic of interest and concern for more than two decades, but the phrase itself is misleading. Cyber operations - the ability to remotely manipulate computer networks - have created a new military capability. The internet and computers provide cyber tools and techniques that counties use for influence, coercion and, potentially, attack. Militaries will use cyber attacks to disrupt command and control, manipulate software, degrade weapons performance and produce political or psychological effect.

Most cyber "attacks" will not produce destructive effects similar to kinetic weapons, but will instead seek to disrupt data and services, create confusion, damage networks and computers (including software and computers embedded in weapons systems) and perhaps destroy machinery. Cyber attacks could strike military, government and perhaps civilian targets, such as critical infrastructure in the opponent homeland.

Advanced cyber attacks can produce effects equivalent to an attack using a bomb or missile, but this is not the most likely use. Cyber attacks that produce military effect can include the manipulation of software, data, knowledge, and opinion to degrade performance and produce political or psychological effect. Since most modern weapons depend on software for their performance, an ability to damage or degrade weapons system software can provide real military advantage by making the weapons inoperable or by degrading their performance.

We should not interpret cyber war solely from the perspective of physical damage. Command and control networks are an important target and attacks on them need not produce physical damage. The Russian penetration of Central Command's classified networks in 2008 showed that Russia, who is our most skilled opponent, would probably try to disrupt command and control in the event of a crisis. Similarly, China penetrating the networks of U.S. Transportation Command and its contractors to test the ability to disrupt American power projection capabilities by interrupting deployments and supply efforts. The absence of physical damage complicates the application of international law.

No non-state actor has acquired or developed the capabilities for a cyber attack that could cause physical damage or casualties. In fact, only a few nations now possess these capabilities. Non-state actors use cyberspace for recruitment, training, fund-raising and proselytizing, not to exert force. Non-state actors have used cyber attacks for coercive purposes, such as denial of service attacks or leaks of damaging information. These actions do not qualify as the use of force but give non-state actors new tools for coercion. Non-state actors like Hezbollah, Hamas or ISIS have not yet used cyber attacks, but Iran may be supporting Hezbollah and Hamas in developing such capabilities for use against Israel.

What this means is that our major opponents are likely to only launch damaging cyber attacks (e.g. those with effects equivalent to a kinetic attack) in the event of armed conflict with the United States. Outside of armed conflict, the primary state use of will be cyber espionage and cyber actions intended to coerce (such as in Estonia or with Sony) that fall below the level of the use of force.

True cyber attacks (e.g. those that inflict physical damage) have been rare, but that does not mean we should dismiss their risk. Most major militaries are developing cyber attack capabilities. Cyber attack will be part of any future war. For the U.S., all of our most likely opponents in any armed conflict – Russia, China, Iran and North Korea – have developed cyber attack capabilities and have engaged in cyber reconnaissance against U.S. military targets and critical infrastructure to prepare for possible attack. We have done the same to them.

Cyber attacks against critical infrastructure could disrupt vital services and possible cause physical destruction, but only a few major powers have this capability and they have been very cautious in using it. How a country uses cyber techniques is determined by its interests, strategies, experience, institutions, and its perceptions of and tolerance for risk. This means that critical infrastructure is a target for cyber attack as it was a target for nuclear missiles, but will only be attacked when an opposing state finds itself in a conflict wish the U.S.

This spread of attack capabilities makes cybersecurity is an increasingly important problem for collective self-defense. In the last few years, the U.S. has worked with its allies to create structures and capabilities for collective cyber defense and has amended collective defense treaties with NATO, Australia and Japan to expand their application to include cyber attacks. NATO's September 2014 summit established that cyber defence is part of the Alliance's core tasks of collective defence, crisis management, and cooperative security. Consistent with its defensive mission, NATO emphasizes "prevention, detection, resilience, recovery." Japan has made significant strides to improve its cybersecurity posture in the last few years, but cybersecurity remains an area of vulnerability for Japan and the bilateral security alliance. The place of cybersecurity in mutual defense is linked to the larger constitutional debate in Japan over the role of the armed forces and redefining the scope of self-defense. Moving forward, alliance relationships will require both greater cooperation and greater effort in cybersecurity.

Since 2007, the U.S. has also developed a framework of policy, doctrine and operational concepts for the use of offensive cyber operations. This framework embeds cyber operations in the existing structure of rules that apply to military and intelligence operations. Cyber actions are approved by the President under Title 50 or Title 10, authorities for intelligence or the use of military force, in consultation with the committees of jurisdiction. In the next year, we should also expect to see greater use of "countermeasures" (such as indictment and sanctions) that do not involve the use of force and which do not require further Congressional assent.

The U.S. has engaged in offensive cyber actions, largely in Afghanistan and Iraq, under the existing Authorization for the Use of Military Force. These have not been attacks in the kinetic sense but the manipulation of opponent command and control networks. A hypothetical example might be the penetration of an insurgent communication network to tell a commander that it is safe to move in a certain direction when in fact he is moving into a U.S. ambush. There are also public allegations, the most salient being Stuxnet, that the U.S. has engaged cyber attacks under intelligence authorities.

Deterrence in Cyberspace

Despite having demonstrated capabilities in cyber defense, the U.S. has obtained little or no deterrent benefit from them. A number of issues complicate and limit the utility of deterrence for cyber security. Deterrence is the threat to use force in retaliation for an attack. We cannot deter cyber crime or espionage. New opponents have a greater tolerance for risk and have planned their actions to avoid triggering U.S. deterrent responses. International law and norms define when force can be used in self-defense and require that it be proportional to the attack. China knows that espionage has never justified a military response. Iran may wonder how many bank websites it needs to disrupt to trigger retaliation. Equally important, an inability to make credible threats makes cyber deterrence ineffective. Within the limits of its applicability, because deterrence will not shield us from most malicious cyber actions, the best way the U.S. could improve deterrence would be to increase its ability to make credible threats.

International law and State practice do not define espionage or crime as attacks that justify the use of force in response. Deterrence will not work against these activities. Cyber deterrence faced a crisis this year. This crisis grew out of a string of failures for "extended deterrence," including our inability to deter Russia in Crimea, to deter ISIS or the Assad Regime in Syria, and on a lesser scale, a failure to deter the attacks on Sony, the Sands Casino, and Github.

In this context, it is difficult to make credible threats. Our opponents plan their operations in ways that circumvent deterrence. They look for tactics to manage and reduce risk and stay below the implicit thresholds of use of force or armed attack that allow them to damage the U.S. without triggering retaliation. While we can be confident that our nuclear and conventional superiority will deter major attacks on the U.S. and its allies, it will not deter malicious cyber activities. The ineffectiveness of deterrence increases the need for international agreement on norms and the application of international law

The Administration's response to the Sony incident had the effect of improving cyber deterrence. The public attention given to improved U.S. ability to attribute an attack may have made the DPRK (and others, such as Iran and China) more cautious in considering cyber attacks against U.S. targets, and the creation of new cyber sanctions (and an apparent willingness to use them) has helped to change opponent risk calculus.

That said, we cannot rely on deterrence and need to rethink its place in cybersecurity and our larger national strategies. We have not deterred cyber espionage or cyber crime. Our opponents do not want to start a war with the U.S., but they do not fear starting a war over spying or cyber crime. Deterrence requires opponents to compare the benefits of an action against the potential cost and assess the likelihood that such costs will actually be imposed. There must be credible threats or actual retaliation if deterrence is to work.

The experience of sanctions and indictments show that there are alternatives to the threat to use military force to deter malicious cyber activities, including espionage and crime. These actions change the opponent calculus and fall in the general category of "countermeasures," retaliatory actions not involving the use of force that are considered legitimate under international law. Countermeasures are important because so far, our opponents have faced no cost and little risk in carrying out malicious cyber actions.

For example, eighteen months ago the U.S. indicted five PLA officers for cyber espionage. At the time, many commentators saw indictment as a waste of time as the five would never go to trial. But the Chinese hated the indictments, and the experience of indictments reinforced the threat of potential U.S. sanctions in ways that helped the U.S. and China reach agreement on cybersecurity. The Chinese did not want to re-experience the pain of indictments as a result of any sanctions. While that agreement has yet to be tested, and while sanctions for China IP theft through cyber espionage are still possible, countermeasures not involving the use of force may be more effect in deterring cyber espionage and crime.

What is the role of diplomacy in containing cyber conflict?

The first use of cyber attack for military purposes occurred in the mid 1990s, when the U.S. used primitive cyber attack tools against Serbia. In the late 1990s, Chinese military writings discussed cyber attack as a means to gain asymmetric advantage over the United States. Perhaps this led Russia to propose in the UN in 1998 a treaty to limit the development and use of cyber weapons. The draft treaty drew on Russia's experience with Strategic Arms control, but it was unworkable, largely designed to hobble the U.S., and did not receive much support. However, the Russian proposal began a process of international negotiation that has now produced results.

With the failure of its treaty proposal, Russia called for the UN to create a Group of Government Experts – GGE) to study the problem of cybersecurity and make recommendations on measures to reduce risk and increase stability. A first GGE in 2003 failed to reach agreement. The second GGE (2010) produced a short report that called on the international community to develop norms and confidence building measures (CBMs) and to build cybersecurity capacity in developing countries. This short report created the agenda for international discussion for cybersecurity. A more extensive GGE Report in 2013 changed the Internet's political landscape by agreeing that the national sovereignty, the UN Charter and international law applied in cyberspace to the same degree they apply in the physical world. This agreement got rid of 1990s ideas that hampered negotiations, such as the idea that cyberspace was a borderless global commons, and the application of sovereignty and international law embeds cyberspace and cybersecurity in the existing framework of international relations that government conducts among states.

The U.S. plays a leading role in the work of the GGE. Its diplomatic strategy for cybersecurity is based on the developing cooperative measures, norms or responsible state behavior in cyberspace and confidence building measures (CBMs). Norms reflect the international community's expectations about behavior. Unlike a treaty, norms are not legally binding, but experience shows they are useful. A norms-based approach offers the greatest chance for progress. There are already implicit norms governing cyber conflict that are derived from existing international law and practice. The argument that norms are too weak can be dismissed as there is no serious alternative.

CBMs focus on transparency and coordination. Voluntarily measures agreed ad ref in the Organization for Security Cooperation in Europe (OSCE), which has played a leading role in the development of CBMs, include the provision of national views on cyber doctrine, strategy, and threats. OSCE members will also share information on national organizations, programs, or strategies relevant to cybersecurity, identify a contact point to facilitate communications and dialogue on ICT-security matters, and establish links between national CERTS. OSCE members discussed how existing OSCE mechanisms, such as the OSCE Communications Network, could be used to facilitate communications on cybersecurity incidents and develop additional measures to reduce the risk of misunderstanding.

The most recent GGE, which concluded in June of this year, was tasked by the UN to identify the application of international law, the development of norms and CBMS, and to further progress on measures to promote capacity building, as the core elements of an international approach to stability and security in cyberspace. In the negotiations, the most difficult of these topics turned out to be the application of international law, as countries were unable to agree on what qualifies as the use of force in cyberspace. Despite this, the 2015 GGE was able to agree on an expanded set of norms and CBMs (modeled loosely on the work of the OSCE) and on the application of international law.

A review of the applicability of existing law of armed conflict suggests that if we approach cyber warfare as a new military technology, existing international law can be largely applied to cyber conflict, but the central obstacle to this is the lack of agreement as to what should be considered the use of force or armed attack in cyberspace. Common understandings on the use of force and armed attack are fundamental both for applying the laws of armed conflict and for modernizing the mutual defense alliances the U.S. has with its allies.

The crux of the disagreement is over UN Charter Article 2/3, which call upon members to renounce the use of force to settle conflict, and Article 51, with reiterates member states inherent right of self defense against armed attack. These ambiguities, however, are not unique to cyber conflict, date from the signing of the Charter, and reflect conflicting desires to renounce the use of force while preserving the right to use force in self-defense.

There is no agreement on what qualifies as the use of force (2/4) and armed attack (51), but there appear to be implicit understanding on these concepts, albeit imprecise. These implicit understandings probably reflect nations understandings of risk; attacks that cause physical damage or casualties are more likely to qualify as the use of force and justify retaliation. Cyber attacks equivalent in effect to kinetic attacks. The area of greatest ambiguity involves cyber attacks that do not produce physical damage or casualties but do involve damage. Examples would include the hacking of Sony by North Korea or on Aramco by Iran. These concepts, use of force and armed attack have major implications for cyber war and for U.S. alliance commitments on mutual defense (which, for the US, are predicated on language that reflects Articles 2/4 and 51).

Continued ambiguity over the application of these UN Charter articles serves the interests of Russia and China by not creating grounds for legitimizing retaliation for cyber actions. This includes a general rejection of Western efforts to define "use of force" and "armed attack" using the concepts of equivalence and effect. The Russian and Chinese goal, similar to other arms control negotiations by these countries, is to constrain the U.S. and its allies.

While the GGE is the most important negotiating venue for multilateral negotiations, there are also important efforts in the Organization for Security Cooperation in Europe, the Organization of

American States, the ASEAN Regional Forum, and in the "London Process," a multilateral effort whose April 2015 meeting in the Netherlands produced valuable results for cooperation, confidence building, and the development of norms. There is also continued effort to increase support for the Budapest Convention, a formal treaty on cyber crime that "normalizes" cyberspace by defining state responsibilities for enforcement and cooperation, but the Convention has made slow progress in the face of opposition from Russia and other countries, reinforcing the point that there is too much distrust among competing nations for formal global agreement.

Next Steps for Congress and the Administration

Congressional oversight and guidance for cybersecurity is spread among a number of committees, including intelligence, armed services, homeland security and others. The foreign affairs committees, in contrast, have played a lesser role. Given the importance of cybersecurity and the internet for security, commerce and international stability, this should change. The areas for specific attention include:

- Oversight of diplomatic actions and negotiations, including implementation and compliance of alliance commitment and bilateral agreements, such as the recent agreement with China;
- Legislative action to strengthen law enforcement and countermeasures for cyber crime and cyber espionage;
- Greater clarity on the legislative basis for authorizing the use of force in cyberspace;
- The development and review of international strategies for cyber security.

This administration was the first to put in place an international strategy. The 2011 international strategy for cybersecurity aims to build cooperation among countries and reaching agreement on cybersecurity norms and confidence building measures (CBMs). The central goal of the strategy is agreement on norms for responsible state behavior in cyberspace.

Given the very different international environment we now face, the U.S. need to reconsider and revise this strategy. The fundamental point for reconsideration is whether to pursue global agreement on cybersecurity norms for responsible state behavior, or begin by building consensus among like-minded nations. While both approaches can be pursued simultaneously, a new strategy will need to examine different kinds of engagements with other countries and a broader range of tools to win progress. It would continue to pursuit of global agreement but seek immediate agreement among like-minded nations on responsible behavior in cyberspace. These understandings should be reinforced by countermeasures and credible threats to encourage responsible behavior and strengthen the rule of law in cyberspace.

Cybersecurity is the product of larger security and trade issues that shape the international agenda. It poses difficult challenges for foreign policy and international security. In this, it is essential that Congress update its understanding of the problem to giver the international and diplomatic aspects of cybersecurity their appropriate weight. I thank the Committee for the opportunity to testify and will be happy to answer any questions.

Mr. SALMON. Dr. Lotrionte.

STATEMENT OF CATHERINE LOTRIONTE, PH.D., DIRECTOR, IN-STITUTE FOR LAW, SCIENCE AND GLOBAL SECURITY, GEORGETOWN UNIVERSITY

Ms. LOTRIONTE. Thank you for the invitation to speak to you today about international law and cyber operations.

Even though there have not yet been discrete cyber operations that rise to the level of damage to property and lives equivalent to kinetic attacks, cyber operations are a part of the traditional military operations today, fast becoming a part of modern kinetic warfare. Such cyber operations first appeared overtly in the 2008 armed conflict between Georgia and Russia, also during the armed conflicts in Afghanistan and Iraq, and throughout the armed conflict in Libya and Syria, and recently have played a significant role during the 2014 armed conflict between Russia and Ukraine.

This emerging reality requires that states examine the question of how to treat cyber operations under international law. There appears no alternative at present but to consider a host of legal propositions in examining the law related to cyber operations and assessing whether the laws that we currently have are adequate as cyber operations become ubiquitous.

Under current international law, cyber operations would amount to internationally wrongful acts if they were inconsistent with established international law. To date, there is only one treaty that explicitly addresses cyber activities: That is the 2001 Budapest Convention on cyber crime.

There is a growing international consensus that aspects of international law do apply in the cyber domain, but most of the details about how it applies remains in flux. Many states have affirmed the application of existing laws, including the U.N. Charter and the Laws of Armed Conflict. And while it is well settled in the U.S. that the U.N. Charter and the Laws of Armed Conflict apply to cyber warfare, the challenge is determining exactly how it applies and getting international agreement on those issues.

In July of this year, the fourth U.N. Group of Government Experts, under the auspices of the Secretary General and composed of 20 states, finalized its recent report to the General Assembly. The report highlighted norms for peacetimes that states should abide by, including that states should not conduct or knowingly support actions that intentionally damage critical infrastructure of other states.

Under the international law related to the use of force, it remains unclear whether a cyber operation that does not result in physical damage or injury can nevertheless amount to an armed attack for purposes of Article 51 of the U.N. Charter, when it generates severe but nondestructive or injurious effects.

While the U.S. has asserted in a report to the U.N. that "under certain circumstances a disruptive activity in cyberspace could constitute an armed attack," it has not indicated which sorts of disruptive activities would qualify.

And under International Humanitarian Law, or IHL, cyber operations executed in the context of an armed conflict are subject to the Law of Armed Conflict. For example, because the conflict between Russia and the Ukraine is international in nature, the ensuing cyber operations are subject to IHL. However, for the customary legal rules of proportionality and the requirement to take certain precautions during an attack under IHL, the meaning of the word ''attack'' for purposes of cyber operations is contested, and yet it is critically important in determining if the rules apply.

In conclusion, while there may never be a comprehensive treaty on cyber operations under international law, verbal acts, such as diplomatic statements, policy statements, press releases, military manuals, decisions of national courts, opinions of official legal advisors, pleadings before international tribunals, and executive decisions and regulations, and importantly for this committee, domestic legislation can also serve to develop customary international law.

The U.S. can actively work to develop these specific customary principles that it wishes to prevail internationally by being outspoken and transparent about what it views as the law in cyberspace. This, of course, will also require constant and consistent action along with those words.

Given the existing difficulties involved with adopting a new treaty in this area, a reinterpretation of existing laws to accord with the emergence of cyber operations, along with the development of new customs that serve to adapt existing norms to cyber operations, will likely be the path states take.

The U.S. can build deterrence by telegraphing or clearly articulating and promulgating an interpretation of the law it believes is applicable to cyber operations. Doing this means being specific and being clear, specifically about the thresholds for a use of force and an armed attack under the law. For example, on the issue of what constitutes a use of force, the U.S. could take the position that cyber operations executed against certain categories of targets, whether they are SCADA systems or specific critical infrastructures, creates a rebuttable presumption that such actions constitute a use of force for purposes of Article 2 of the U.N. Charter.

The U.S. could explicitly state such a position is a White House national security strategy, for instance. In making such legal assertions regarding thresholds and acting in accordance with those outlined thresholds, the U.S. could also seek agreement on these explicit thresholds from other States to develop clearly what the law is. Under such a legal framework, we can develop methods of countermeasures to hold those accountable for not complying with the law. This is just one way to develop deterrence when speaking about cyber conflict.

I thank you, and I look forward to your questions.

Mr. SALMON. Thank you.

[The prepared statement of Ms. Lotrionte follows:]

Prepared Testimony and
Statement for the Record of

**Catherine Lotrionte
Professor, Georgetown University**

Hearing on

"Cyber War: Definitions, Deterrence, and Foreign Policy"

Before the

House Committee on Foreign Affairs

September 30, 2015

2172 Rayburn House Office Building

Chairman Royce, Ranking Member Engel, Members of the Committee, thank you for the invitation to offer this Statement for the Record on International Law and Cyber Operations.

Introduction

Even though there has not yet been discrete cyber operations that rise to the level of damage to property and lives equivalent to kinetic attacks, cyber operations are a part of the traditional military operations today, fast becoming a part of modern kinetic warfare. Such cyber operations first appeared overtly in the 2008 armed conflict between Georgia and Russia, were employed during the armed conflicts in Afghanistan and Iraq, figured in operations throughout the armed conflict in Libya and Syria and have played a significant role during the 2014 armed conflict between Russia and Ukraine. The United States has established US Cyber Command to conduct defensive and offensive cyber operations during armed conflicts and other states are following suit by developing cyber capabilities and establishing their force structures to leverage them.

According to a 2013 UN study, 32 states included cyberwarfare in their military planning and organizations. And intelligence reports have noted that more than 140 countries have funded cyber weapon development programs. Cyber operations have already become an integral part of command, control, communications, computer, intelligence, surveillance, and reconnaissance (C4ISR) activities in the battlespace and it is inevitable that they will soon play a central role in "attacking" the enemy. The ability to develop these cyber capabilities is also not limited to regular armed forces and states. Non-state actors have also discovered the value of cyber operations as a means of asymmetric warfare.

This emerging reality requires that states examine the question of how to treat cyber operations under international law. There appears no alternative at present but to consider a host of legal propositions in examining the law related to cyber operations and assess whether the laws that we currently have are adequate as cyber operations become ubiquitous. My statement will focus mainly on two areas of international law that are implicated by cyber operations, *jus ad bellum* and *jus in bello*.

The Applicability of International Law to Cyber Operations Conducted by States

Under international law, "war" is not a meaningful term. The existence of a "war" does not trigger *jus ad bellum* provisions of international law nor is it a necessary trigger for the laws of armed conflict. What is relevant, for purposes of determining the applicability of international law to cyber operations, is to understand the thresholds for "uses of force," "armed attack" and the existence of an "armed conflict" under international law.

Public international law is by nature a dynamic creature that evolves over time through consent of states. The content of this body of law, its interpretation and application develop over time in response to changes in the security environment in which it applies. International law is created by states in two ways: 1) states opting into treaty regimes and 2) state practice that occurs out of a sense of legal obligation (*opinio juris*) or customary international law. For purposes of cyber operations, both *jus ad bellum* and *jus in bello* will have to adapt to the growing threats and new technologies within cyberspace in order to effectively regulate state behavior in this new domain.

Under current international law, cyber operations would amount to internationally wrongful acts if they were inconsistent with established international law. To date, there is only one treaty that explicitly addresses cyber activities: the 2001 Budapest Convention on Cybercrime that requires the state parties to criminalize certain cyber offences in their domestic legislation and to provide mutual assistance in investigations and prosecutions. The lack of treaties and customary international law explicitly addressing cyber operations involving the use of force, however, does not mean that cyber operations can be conducted by states without restrictions.

Cyber operations that amount to a use of force or to acts of hostilities would fall within the provisions of international law that regulate the right of states to use force (*jus ad bellum*) and the conduct of warfare once an armed conflict has broken out (*jus in bello*, also called the laws of armed conflict, LOAC, and international humanitarian law, IHL). In the absence of a specific treaty regulating cyber operations, the question is *whether* and *how* existing treaties and customs that apply to traditional uses of force can be extended to cyber operations. Today, there is a growing international consensus that aspects of international law do apply to the cyber domain but most of the details about how it applies remains in flux.

The key *jus ad bellum* and *jus in bello* treaties are the 1945 Charter of the United Nations, the Hague Conventions of 1899 and 1907, the four 1949 Geneva Conventions on the Protection of Victims of War and their two 1977 Additional Protocols (even though the US is not a party to either). Although these treaties do not mention cyber issues, many states have affirmed the application of existing laws, including the UN Charter and the laws of armed conflict, to cyber operations, usually not distinguishing between treaties and customary international law. Needless to say, states can always conclude less than universal treaties, or even special bi-lateral agreements to expand their obligations under existing international law, *jus ad bellum* and *jus in bello*. Such agreements may be concluded in relation to a particular conflict, or to submit to special protection certain data or critical infrastructure. For example, in the future, there may develop agreement between certain states that cyber operations against essential civilian services, data and critical infrastructure constitute "attacks" under IHL and thereby those states will refrain from conducting such "attacks" and condemn those that conduct them.

In a speech at the US Cyber Command in 2010, the then-legal advisor of the US State Department, Harold Koh, emphasized that international law principles do apply in cyberspace, including but not limited to the *jus ad bellum* and the *jus in bello*. The 2011 White House *International Strategy for Cyberspace* explained that '[t]he development of norms for state conduct in cyberspace does not require a reinvention of customary international law, nor does it render existing international norms obsolete.' While it is well-settled in the US that the UN Charter and the laws of armed conflict apply to cyber warfare, the challenge is determining exactly *how* it applies and getting international agreement on those issues. As noted in the Department of Defense's *Law of War Manual*, released in June 2015, "[p]recisely how the law of war applies to cyber operations is not well-settled..." While there appears to be growing consensus that cyber operations do not exist in a legal or normative vacuum, the law is still in flux and will likely continue to evolve in the future as state practice and *opinio juris* exposes common ground between states as states recognize the shared benefits to agreement on the law.

In 2013, the third Group of Governmental Experts on Developments in the Field of Information and Telecommunications in the Context of International Security (UN GGE), established under the auspices of the UN Secretary-General and composed of 15 states, including the US, Russian and China,[1] established agreement on recommendations in its final report on norms, rules, and principles for responsible behaviour of States as well as confidence-building measures and capacity-building. The report affirmed the applicability of international law to cyberspace (explicitly citing the UN Charter); stressing that states must meet their international obligations regarding international wrongful acts attributable to them; states should not use proxies to conduct wrongful acts; and should ensure that their territories are not used by non-state actors for unlawful use of Information and Communications Technologies (ICTs).

In July of this year, the fourth UN GGE, composed of 20 states,[2] finalized its report to the General Assembly. The report highlighted norms for peacetime that states should abide by, including, states should not conduct or knowingly support actions that intentionally damage critical infrastructures of other states; states should assist in requests from other states when their critical infrastructure has been attacked; states should not conduct or support any harmful actions against the information systems of emergency response teams; and states should seek to prevent the proliferation of malicious ICT tools. The report also reiterated the recommendations of the prior UN GGEs, supporting the applicability of international legal obligations in cyberspace, state responsibility for attributable wrongful acts

---

[1] Additional member states of the 3rd UN GGE were: Argentina, Australia, Belarus, Canada, Egypt, Estonia, France, Germany, India, Indonesia, Japan and the United Kingdom of Great Britain and Northern Ireland.

[2] List of the 20 states in the 4th UN GGE: Belarus, Brazil, China, Colombia, Egypt, Estonia, France, Germany, Ghana, Israel, Japan, Kenya, Malaysia, Mexico, Pakistan, Republic of Korea, Russian Federation, Spain, United Kingdom of Great Britain and Northern Ireland, United States.

and the obligation to prevent their state's territory from being used to conduct wrongful acts in cyberspace.

In 2013, a group of twenty international legal experts, who had been convened under the auspices of the NATO Cyber Defence Centre of Excellence in Tallinn, Estonia, published the *Tallinn Manual on the International Law of Cyber Warfare*, which examined the implications under *jus ad bellum* and *jus in bello* of cyber warfare. The Manual includes a set of 95 Rules accompanied by commentaries and while it does not reflect NATO doctrine or the official position of any state or organization, it is a good starting point for further analysis on what international laws are applicable to cyber operations.

Use of Force (Jus ad Bellum)

The *jus ad bellum* determines when states may lawfully resort to force in international relations. It is distinction from the *jus in bello* which governs how force may be used once an armed conflict has commenced. In 1945 the UN Charter, in articles 2(4) and 51, redefined previously accepted ideas of *jus ad bellum* and codified the contemporary *jus ad bellum* in its entirety. Article 2(4) states: "All Members shall refrain in their international relations from the threat or use of force against the territorial integrity or political independence of any State, or in any other manner inconsistent with the Purposes of the United Nations." If a state activity is a use of force within the meaning of Article 2(4), it is unlawful under international law. There are two exceptions in the UN Charter to this general prohibition on the use of force: (1) uses of force authorized by the UN Security Council pursuant to Article 42 of the Charter and (2) individual and collective self-defense in response to an "armed attack" pursuant to Article 51 of the Charter.

Before the advent of cyber operations, states and scholars struggled to define the threshold at which an act becomes a "use of force." Over time, states sought to include a broader range of acts within the meaning of a use of force including acts that would not necessarily be armed but that had aggressive intent. During the 1960s, however, the predominant opinion confined the term to direct uses of or threats to use armed force with aggressive intent justifying defensive military action. It is notable, however, that article 2(4) does not use the word "armed" in reference to force. Today, there is a general understanding that uses of force do not necessarily have to be actions conducted by a state's armed forces to constitute a use of force. It is also accepted that actions involving economic coercion and espionage would fall below the threshold of a use of force. Most international legal scholars today accept that in analyzing actions that may rise to the level of a use of force consideration should be given to the "scale and effects" of the actions rather than focusing solely on whether it involved armed action by a state's forces. In the *Nicaragua* case the International Court of Justice rejected a narrow interpretation of "use of force" that would limit the term to the use of either kinetic force or non-kinetic operations generating comparable effects.

Since the emergence of cyber operations, states and scholars have struggled to define the threshold at which an act in cyberspace would constitute a "use of force" for purposes of Article 2(4) of the Charter. The main challenge in determining whether a cyber operation would be a use of force has been in the application of the rule to cyber operations that, on the one hand, produce severe non-physical consequences but, on the other, do not use destructive or injurious force. Given the lack of a definitive criteria for characterizing an act, in general, as a use of force under international law, it is not surprising that there would be challenges with characterizing cyber operations as uses of force.

Accepting the reasoning of the *Nicaragua* case, the Tallinn Manual adopted an approach concentrating on an act's "scale and effects." (Rule 11 of the Tallinn Manual). This is the same approach articulated in the armed attack context in the *Nicaragua* case. Notice was also taken in the Manual of the discussions at the 1945 UN Charter drafting conference during which economic coercion was regarded by states as not constituting a use of force. Relying on the *Nicaragua* judgment, the Tallinn Manual concluded that non-destructive cyber operations may sometimes amount to a use of force. For example, according to the Manual, while merely funding a hactivist group that is conducting cyber operations, as part of an insurgency, would not qualify as a use of force, arming and training an organized armed group to carry out cyber operations against another state would.

Article 51 of the UN Charter addresses when states may use force in self-defense in response to cyber operations that constitute armed attacks. In line with the *Nicaragua* Court that drew a distinction between uses of forces and armed attacks, the Tallinn Manual concluded that the term "armed attack" differs from "use of force." Only the most grave "uses of force" through cyber operations, the Tallinn Manual experts held, would amount to an "armed attack" triggering the right of a state to use a forcible self-defense measure.[3] The experts agreed that any cyber operation that injures or kills persons or damages or destroys property amounts to an armed attack. The required degree of damage or injury, however, remains the subject of much disagreement. Furthermore, in applying traditional customary principles to cyber operations, any response in self-defense against cyber operations or kinetic attacks amounting to an armed attack, must meet the requirements of necessity, proportionality and immediacy.

Both Harold Koh in his speech and DoD's Law of War Manual apply this traditional "scale and effects" test to the analysis of what would be a use of force or armed attack in cyberspace. According to both, if the physical damage or results of cyber operations were the same as kinetic acts of dropping bombs or firing a missile then the right of self-defense is triggered and traditional laws of war principles of humanity, suffering, injury or destruction unnecessary to accomplish a legitimate

---

[3] Since the *Nicaragua* decision, the US had rejected the Court's holding that there is a gap between the thresholds for uses of force and armed attacks. In his 2010 speech, Harold Koh reiterated this US position as it applies to cyber operations.

military purpose must be avoided in cyber operations. While the 2015 UN GGE report mentions the language of Article 2(4), it does not provide any detail about possible thresholds and the Russians have indicated that there was disagreement among the member states as to whether Article 51 even applies to cyber operations.

So, while there have been attempts at gaining agreement among states related to how *jus ad bellum* is implicated in cyber operations, uncertainty remains as to where the thresholds for uses of force and armed attacks lie. For example, it remains unclear whether a cyber operation that does not result in physical damage or injury can nevertheless amount to an armed attack, for purposes of Article 51, when it generates severe nondestructive or injurious effects. While the US has asserted in a report to the UN that "under some circumstances, a disruptive activity in cyberspace could constitute an armed attack,"[4] it has not indicated which sorts of disruptive activities would qualify.

International Humanitarian Law (IHL) (Jus in Bello)

Cyber operations conducted by belligerents against each other after the initiation of "hostilities" or a "declaration of war" are regulated by the relevant *jus in bello* provisions, whether or not kinetic hostilities occur. This body of international law regulates *how* hostilities may be conducted in armed conflict and *protects* those affected by them. The international treaties that are relevant are the Geneva and Hague conventions as well as customary international legal principles of distinction, necessity, humanity, and proportionality. It is worth noting that declarations of war have not been issued in any recent conflict. The very notion of "war" as an international legal concept has been replaced by the term 'armed conflict'. In the information age, declarations of war are even more unlikely to occur. Requiring a declaration of war would appear to be unrealistic as it is not reconcilable with the surprise and plausible deniability factors that constitute two of the main advantages of cyber operations.

Cyber operations, however, executed in the context of an armed conflict (both international and non-international armed conflict) are subject to the law of armed conflict. For example, because the conflict between Russia and the Ukraine is international in character, the ensuing cyber operations are subject to IHL. According to the International Committee of the Red Cross (ICRC), the 'means and methods of warfare which resort to cyber technology are subject to IHL just as any new weapon or delivery system has been so far when used in an armed conflict by or on behalf of a party to such conflict.' The ICRC has noted that all parties to a conflict have an obligation to respect the rules of international humanitarian law if they resort to means and methods of cyberwarfare, including the principles of distinction, proportionality and precaution. The 2015 UN GGE report also noted

---

[4] Rep. of the Secretary-General, Developments in the Field of Information and Telecommunications in the Context of International Security, U.N. Doc. A/66/152, at 18 (July 20, 2010).

that the customary legal principles of IHL, humanity, necessity, proportionality and distinction apply in cyberspace.[5]

The question remains, however, as to whether isolated cyber operations between states without concurrent traditional hostilities will be regarded as amounting to an armed conflict, thereby triggering the laws of armed conflict. In other words, can cyber operations along constitute armed conflict? This question will probably be determined only through future state practice. Even the team of experts for the Tallinn Manual were unable to find agreement on this question. Providing some relevant insight on this question, the *Nicaragua* Court held that "clearly, use of force may *in some circumstances* raise questions of [IHL] law," implying that not always does a use of armed force amount to an armed conflict and thus trigger the application of *jus in bello*. For example, the mere supplying of arms to rebels does not bring about a state of war in the material sense. However, if a state not only armed the rebels but also trained them, it would be 'waging war' against the state fought by the rebels. Furthermore, other violations of Article 2(4) of the UN Charter, such as measures involving the threat but not the use of armed force (quarantine) also do not initiate, in themselves, an international armed conflict.

The Tallinn Manual accepts this view, stating that '[a]n international armed conflict exists whenever there are hostilities, which may include or be limited to cyber operations, occurring between two or more States,' where 'hostilities' is intended as 'the collective application of means and methods of warfare.' In order to qualify as a 'means of warfare', for example, any software deployed must be able to 'injure the enemy.' According to Michael Schmitt, who was the project director of the Tallinn Manual, IHL 'applies whenever computer network attacks can be ascribed to a State, are more than merely sporadic and isolated incidents and are either intended to cause injury, death, damage or destruction (or analogous effects), or such consequences are foreseeable.' The question is unsettled as to what level of damage must be met to trigger an armed conflict. For example, there is no consensus as to whether cyber operations resulting in severe non-destructive and non-injurious consequences can qualify as hostilities.

For the customary rules of proportionality and the requirement to take certain precautions during an attack, the meaning of the work 'attack' for purposes of cyber operations is contested and yet critically important to determining if the rules apply. Much debate has taken place among scholars and the Tallinn Manual experts on the issue, with no unanimous agreement. The question is whether the term "attack" is limited to that which causes physical harm to persons or intangible objects or whether is applies to acts of interference with the functionality of an object. The question of how states will realize the protection of certain objects or persons from cyber operations in an armed conflict is likely to develop over time. It is unlikely

---

[5] List of the 20 states in the 4th UN GGE: Belarus, Brazil, China, Colombia, Egypt, Estonia, France, Germany, Ghana, Israel, Japan, Kenya, Malaysia, Mexico, Pakistan, Republic of Korea, Russian Federation, Spain, United Kingdom of Great Britain and Northern Ireland, United States.

that any international agreement will be developed on the issue of banning any cyber operations against civilian activities or data especially when non-destructive psychological operations directed at the civilian population are lawful in traditional kinetic conflict. Indeed, for cyber operations that only cause inconvenience or interference with non-essential services it would be difficult to get international agreement on such a ban. However, states in practice may begin to treat cyber operations against *essential* civilian services and data (financial services) as 'attacks' under LOAC, refraining from targeting them and condemning those that target them. In this manner, state practice may develop into customary international law over time. In other words, state practice will ultimately determine which specific civilian services and data will qualify as essential and therefore off-limits during conflict.

Conclusions

The international laws related to use of force and armed conflict were developed at a time when cyber operations were not even a thought in the minds of the drafters of the relevant treaties. When these rules were promulgated states did not have the capability to carry out cyber operations such as today. Today, however, cyber capabilities proliferate and states view them as force multipliers. These capabilities, however, also represent vulnerabilities for these states that rely on ICTs. Modern warfare has highlighted the need for these international laws to accommodate such capabilities within the law while ensuring that the object and purpose of IHL is protected during hostilities.

With this point in mind, I will offer a couple of thoughts as to where international law may be evolving in the context of cyber operations and the potential role for the US in the development of that law to ensure that the future legal landscape matches with the national security needs of the nation. To start with a claim, there likely will not be a new treaty codified that covers all aspects of the use of cyber operations under international law. In fact, since the path to negotiating any such treaty would be an arduous one, it is likely a waste of time, in my opinion, to attempt to arrive at such an agreement. Customary international law, however, can develop over time through state practice.

Customary international law evolves as states make claims about what they believe the law *is*, and *does*, in specific areas. Verbal acts such as diplomatic statements, policy statements, press releases, military manuals, decisions of national courts, opinions of official legal advisors, pleadings before international tribunals and executive decisions and regulations can all serve to develop international law. The US can actively work to develop those specific customary principles that it wishes to prevail internationally by being outspoken and transparent about what it views as the law in cyberspace. This, of course, will also require action consistent with words. Given the existing difficulties involved with adopting a new treaty, a reinterpretation of existing law to accord with the emergence of cyber operations along with the development of new customs that serve to adapt existing norms to cyber operations will likely be the path states take.

In this regard, it is paramount that the US government considers the importance of taking an active role in publicly setting forth its claims about how international law specifically applies to cyber operations or face the possibility that other states will develop the laws in a manner inconsistent with the interests of this country.

While it is difficult to predict whether any bright line tests will emerge in the areas of jus ad bellum and jus in bello, options for greater clarification of legal thresholds for cyber operations within this body of law exist. The US could articulate and promulgate an interpretation of the law it believes is applicable to cyber operations. For example, on the issue of what constitutes a use of force, the US could take the position that cyber operations executed against certain categories of targets, whether they are SCADA systems or specific critical infrastructures, creates a rebuttable presumption that such actions constitute "uses of force" for purposes of Article 2(4) of the UN Charter. The US could explicitly state such a position in a White House National Security Strategy asserting the legal thresholds for what would constitute a "use of force" and an "armed attack" in cyberspace. In making such legal assertions regarding thresholds, and acting in accordance with those outlined thresholds, the US could also seek agreement on these explicit thresholds from other states.

Mr. SALMON. Mr. Butler.

STATEMENT OF MR. BOB BUTLER, ADJUNCT SENIOR FELLOW, TECHNOLOGY AND NATIONAL SECURITY PROGRAM, CENTER FOR A NEW AMERICAN SECURITY

Mr. BUTLER. Congressman Salmon, Ranking Member Engel, and distinguished members of the committee, thank you again for the invitation to come and talk about cyber war and related topics. These are my opinions and not necessarily those of the U.S. Government or the Center for a New American Security.

The bottom line upfront for me is that, you know, we have done a good job, I think, as a country in building strategy and developing strategy. We are lagging in implementation. And I would agree with my colleagues and Congressman Salmon's remarks about deterrence deficit. We are definitely in a situation of a deterrence deficit, and we are increasing our risk exposure over time by not remedying those actions.

I say this from my perspective as a software developer, that is how I was trained; and from a DOD perspective, where I served in the United States Air Force for 26 years both as a computer systems officer and an intelligence officer; from a policy perspective, having served as a deputy assistant secretary over at the Pentagon on cyber policy; and from 6 years in the private sector working in both building business and building security programs globally.

So rather than going through my remarks, I would just like to summarize some of the salient points and then stand ready for your questions.

First of all, on the topic of cyber war, I think that is a misnomer. We are talking more about actions and tools and capabilities in cyberspace that are used as we move through cyber conflict, and so the idea within the Department of Defense of a combined arms campaign where cyber capabilities are integrated as we go through different phases on the run-up to conflict and de-escalation.

With regards to the treaties, I think Catherine went through it in quite good detail. My sense, and from practical experience, is that the Law of Armed Conflict does apply in cyberspace, as do other international rule sets. There are principles, such as proportionality, that do apply.

Treaties are important. What we have with the North Atlantic Treaty Organization in terms of collective defense is an important aspect of it. And those kinds of treaties that fall below the level of war that we are using in law enforcement, like the Budapest Convention that Dr. Lotrionte mentioned, are key aspects of how we need to think through this problem set.

With regards to deterrence, we have mentioned the International Strategy on Cyberspace a few times. That really is our declaratory statement. We reserve the right to use all means to defend ourselves in accordance with international law. But saying something is not just the only element of deterrence. We need to be able to display and project force, whether that be in economic sanctions or in other ways. We need to have deterrence by denial, where we build up defenses and avoid things like an OPM breach. We need to look at resiliency that takes us beyond U.S. Government activity and into the critical infrastructure. And we need to do more in those areas.

From the standpoint of diplomacy, I think there is definitely a role in this emerging area of cyber diplomacy—whether it be bilateral, multilateral relationships as we see with the North Atlantic Treaty Organization, or multi-stakeholder kinds of partnerships as we talked about with the United Nations and the Government Group of Experts, or in private sector collaboration. More on that in just a few moments.

In terms of foreign policy implications, certainly I think there are foreign policy thrusts here. We need to develop norms. We need to also develop standards and comport to international standards and ensure others comport to those international standards as well. We need to have a leveling set of rules. We need to build partnerships, public-private partnerships that extend internationally, and we need to find enforcement mechanisms as we go forward in time.

In terms of the administration and the assessment that I would have is, again, strategy blueprints have been good, but our implementation has been lagging. We need from the President on down a unified vision and a much greater focus on implementation.

Here we need to look at resources, yes, but also authorities and, more importantly, accountability within each of the departments that have responsibilities here. And I do believe this takes us into new ways of looking at how cyber activities should be comported over time.

In terms of the laws, we need to update the laws, whether it be the existing communications laws, such as the Electronic Communications Privacy Act, the Computer Fraud and Abuse Act, or the Critical Infrastructure Partnership Advisory Council authorities. Those all need to be used as updated tools to help us in this area of building deterrence.

Finally, in terms of the role for the committee, I really endorse Jim Lewis's comment about the committee taking on a greater role in reviewing the International Strategy on Cyberspace. It does need to be updated. The threat has changed significantly. We need measures of effectiveness, and I think it would be helpful for the committee to be involved there.

Secondly, I think as an aspect of that, a key aspect, is to begin to drive international private-public partnerships, to build trust as well as to build a coalition of interested stakeholders to help us with norm development, enforcement of those norms, and understanding of cyber conflict. I think to get to that particular point, it is important to bring in U.S.-based multinational representatives and experts to help inform that discussion and look at things that have been discussed already from the government side, like the Wassenaar agreements on export control.

And then, finally, I think from an education standpoint, there are ways that we can actually increase our understanding through tabletop exercises, and I would commend that the committee think about using such types of tabletop exercises to continue their education and promotion of where they want to go in helping us with cyberspace.

I stand ready to address your questions.

Mr. SALMON. Thank you.

[The prepared statement of Mr. Butler follows:]

Center for a
New American
Security

September 30, 2015

Testimony before the House Foreign Affairs Committee
Cyber War: Definitions, Deterrence, and Foreign Policy

Robert J. Butler, Adjunct Senior Fellow
Center for a New American Security

Mr. Chairman, Ranking Member Engel, and distinguished members of the Committee, thank you for inviting me to speak on the topic of cyber war. I would like to begin by noting that the opinions expressed here today are solely mine and do not reflect the views of any particular organization within or outside the U.S. Government (USG.)

For the last 36 years, my work life has been about Information Technology (IT) and its application across multiple sectors. After graduating with a degree in computer information systems and a focus on quantitative business methods, I began a career in the United States Air Force first as a software developer and then, for the next 26 years, developed or applied information technology as both a computer systems and intelligence officer. Along the way, I was afforded the opportunity to help guide the evolution of information warfare, information and cyberspace strategy and operations within the Department of Defense (DOD) and the USG as a planner and commander. My work in DOD included the stand-up of information operations (IO) organizations, development of IO campaign plans, and serving as the DOD lead in the first USG negotiation with the Russians on cyber arms control in 1998. I was also privileged to serve as the Director of Intelligence at US Transportation Command during Operations Enduring and Iraqi Freedom, just as the Chinese government began aggressive on-line reconnaissance of our critical force projection networks. I culminated my military career by commanding the intelligence operations organization that is now commonly referred to as NSA-Texas.

After retirement from the Air Force, I served as the senior civilian executive for DOD's premiere joint information operations command before joining a US-based global IT services firm as its Director of its Military Intelligence Programs. Returning to government service in 2009, I served as the first Deputy Assistant Secretary of Defense (DASD) for Space and Cyber Policy. My key direction from Defense Secretary Bob Gates and Deputy Secretary Bill Lynn was to get US Cyber Command stood up and write the first DOD cyber strategy. I also had opportunity to provide input and shaping to the first *International Strategy for Cyberspace*. During my time as a DASD, I witnessed and was appalled at the expansion of the cyber threat from China and Russia, especially the rampant on-line theft of US intellectual property by the Chinese and the continued disruptive Russian cyber attacks which was an ominous signal of what was to come from Russia in the Ukraine. I was also dismayed by our struggles to deal effectively with the Wikileaks intrusion and with STUXNET, the world became aware that another threshold had been crossed into the area of cyber-induced physical destruction.

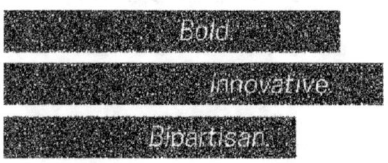

Since leaving government service, I have spent most of my time in the private sector, helping a leading edge data center company, partnered with a very large New York-based financial services firm, "go global" – to Singapore, London and beyond. As the corporate Chief Security Officer, I had the opportunity to build and implement a "bottoms up" security program, countering foreign threats while courting other foreign customers as partners.

From a public sector perspective, I have served as a non-paid senior government expert to the Air Force, Office of the Secretary of Defense and the Department of Homeland Security (DHS) since leaving full-time government service in 2011. Additionally, I serve as a non-resident fellow at the Center for a New American Security. In sum, I believe my technical training, 30 years of DoD experience – in and outside of uniform and my six years in US-based Multinational Corporations, have given me knowledge and insights to address your questions regarding cyber war, deterrence, the role of diplomacy including business diplomacy, foreign policy implications and US actions to date to reduce cyber conflict.

Before addressing these topics, I wanted to give you my perspective on what is meant by cyberspace operations.

- In DOD, we categorize cyberspace operations as computer network operations (CNO), computer network defense (CND), offensive computer operations (OCO) and computer network exploitation (CNE.) Though we (and other militaries) use these categories as an organizing principle, effective cyberspace operations requires the synchronization of all four categories of activities to meet DOD/USG objectives.

- CNO are the actions we take to enable the flow of data from one location to another location; it includes configuring, operating, monitoring and measuring all hardware – from servers to phones, software – operating systems and applications, and networks – whether they are wired or wireless.

- CND are the actions we take to defend the network and more importantly, the information assets and sensitive data we have on the network. CND includes the deployment of technology like firewalls and intrusion detection systems, but also includes organizing concepts like dividing or segmenting networks. Focus for cyber defenders is on ensuring the continuous confidentiality, integrity and availability of the information flowing within an enterprise.

- OCO involves the use of software, hardware and networks to deliver software (malware) for an intended effect against an adversary – usually to disrupt, degrade or destroy an adversary's capability. Targeting is a very difficult process as data may need to flow across multiple "hops" in a network before arriving at the intended target. Along the way, adversaries have opportunity to watch, intercept and/or re-direct. USG has a very detailed system of "checks and balances" prior to approval of an OCO activity.

- CNE is the use of hardware, software and networks to better understand the adversary through collection and analysis of data. CNE is an intelligence activity, integral and necessary to support both CND and OCO activity.

With this context, let me now provide my thoughts on the topics about which you've asked.

Cyber War.

History, other countries' doctrines and technology trends help us to best envision what a future cyber war would like. First off, I believe the term is not especially helpful. We will likely not be involved in a cyber war, but a war that uses cyberspace tools and capabilities to achieve desired effects. That was certainly the case in Estonia, Georgia and Ukraine as Russia prosecuted its campaign to dissuade local ethnic leaders and reverse outcomes considered detrimental to Moscow. As we saw in these Russian incursions, cyberspace operations – both offensive and defensive – were part of a combined arms campaign.

Importantly, I think we need to better understand how cyberspace capabilities could be used in a run-up to war and what we should do to dissuade a potential adversary nation-state. Carrying out an OCO activity requires exquisite intelligence, derived from CNE and other intelligence activities. Capable nation-states would use all of its intelligence, counter-intelligence and other surveillance resources – both on-line and "off net" – to assure highly successful OCO activity. I commend the Defense Science Board (DSB) 2013 report on resiliency for further detail on this subject.

In the run-up to war, an adversary would likely use CNE to surveil our and our allied on-line capabilities, and acquire the needed intelligence for developing battlespace plans – what we call in DOD parlance the Intelligence Preparation of the Battlespace (IPB). Likely targets for CNE would be our command and control (C2) capabilities – especially in our nuclear, missile defense and force projection mission areas, our other military force structures and our nation's commercial critical infrastructure. Implanting of malware in any of these structures by another foreign nation should be a significant cause for concern and warrant NCA action. In deterring and responding to these threats against the US military and the US more broadly, the United States needs a range of credible options. Offensive cyber is necessary, but not sufficient.

International Law and Norms.

From a policy perspective, the Law of Armed Conflict and other International Law apply to the use of force and armed attack. These provisions include the application of proportionality in response. Beyond these laws, NATO provisions obligate us to render assistance to NATO members that have been attacked in cyberspace – as evidence through sustained disruption, degradation and/or destruction of that member nation's C2, other military and/or critical infrastructure. The Tallinn Manual is a good source for further definition of these treaty obligations.

Though not directly applicable to situations of armed attack, the Budapest Convention could also be invoked to render assistance for on-line criminal activity being prosecuted by a nation or criminal group.

Role of Deterrence.

Deterring bad actors' behavior using our cyberspace capabilities is an important and integral aspect of our defense strategy. More importantly, the use of all means – informational, economic, diplomatic, military -- for deterring malicious acts in cyberspace is a critical component of our **International Strategy for Cyberspace**, published by the White House in May of 2011. The recently updated **DoD Cyber Strategy** clearly describes the components of an effective cyber deterrence strategy. First, deterrence must include not only a declaration of response, but a display of effective response capabilities such as the projection of force or sanctions from an economic perspective. Secondly, an effective deterrence strategy must include the development and deployment of effective defense capabilities to deny a potential attack from succeeding. The DOD build-out of the Cyber Mission Force, under Cyber Command leadership, is a foundational element of deterrence by denial. Finally, effective deterrence must incorporate provisions to strengthen the resilience of US systems – C2, other military and commercial critical infrastructure – to withstand attack. Also note that attribution is a fundamental part of an effective cyber deterrence strategy and is enabled through strengthening our intelligence capabilities, and our partnerships with both industry and allies.

Diplomacy in Containing Cyber Conflict.

Proactive diplomacy in cyber conflict is essential to containing cyber conflict. As described in the USG's *International Strategy for Cyberspace*, the USG Executive Branch, under State Department leadership, has been working with other states to build and sustain an open, interoperable, secure and reliable cyberspace environment around the globe, and really creating a new area of foreign policy in the field of cyber diplomacy. The State Department works to meet this diplomatic objective through three activities: bilateral and multilateral partnerships; international and multi-stakeholder organizations; and private sector collaboration. Bilaterally, the US continues to grow capacity building partnerships with the United Kingdom, Australia, Canada, New Zealand, the North Atlantic Treaty Organization, the Gulf Cooperation Council states and allies in the Asia-Pacific region. The USG has been involved for more than a decade in multilateral dialogue with the United Nations' Government Group of Experts to define norms in cyberspace. This year is a notable as there has been consensus among member nations – to include Russia and China – on a small set of norms to include the protection of national critical infrastructure. With the majority of USG critical infrastructure in the hands of US/allied private sector partners, USG collaboration, primarily through DHS, DOD, the Department of Commerce, Department of Treasury, Department of Justice, with US industry – especially US-based MNCs – is a foundational element of US business diplomacy and deterrence.

Foreign Policy Implications.

The Internet is a global platform shared by all states and non-state actors for commercial, humanitarian, defense and other security purposes. As such, the ability to operate in open, interoperable, secure and reliable cyberspace environment is a critical national interest. To achieve that goal, the US must build and sustain an environment in which norms of responsible behavior guide states' actions, sustain partnerships and support the rule of law in cyberspace.

Assessment of US Administration Actions to Date.

The Administration has taken some effective steps in countering and anticipating the threat of conflict in cyberspace facing this nation, but much more needs to be done. The *International Strategy for Cyberspace* and other Departmental Strategies have been good blueprints for what needs to be done and provide the right messaging to the rest of the world for what we should do to effectively operate in cyberspace and reduce cyber conflict. **However, the scale and speed of strategy implementation are lacking and lagging, creating a significant "deterrence deficit" and unacceptable risk exposure for the nation.**

- In order to have credible and effective deterrence of cyber attacks on critical infrastructure by well-resourced adversaries, the U.S. needs to ensure the resilience not only of our nuclear strike capabilities, but of a broader range of non-nuclear capabilities such as conventional strike, missile defense and offensive cyber. In short, we need to do more.

- As noted by the OPM breach, our deterrence by denial across USG systems is not credible. We need to do more.

- As noted in the 2013 DSB report on resiliency and other studies of our grid infrastructure, our resilience, especially in our commercial critical infrastructure, is not at a level to withstand a high-end attack from a determined and resourced adversary. The DSB and other Executive Branch-sponsored reports point to a worsening threat environment which portends for even more trouble. We need to do much more.

So, what should be done?

- The President himself needs to work with you – the Congress – to drive cybersecurity as a national priority --- on level with health care, immigration and the nuclear treaty with Iran.

- We need to back priority with resources and authority to Departmental stakeholders, and hold Departments accountable for rapid action.

- DHS needs resources and authority to autonomically apply "best practice" cyber hygiene across USG agencies.

- DOD needs additional resources to more rapidly build out cyber mission forces and associated infrastructure.

- The White House needs to lead USG efforts to update all cyber-related laws (which are being exploited by adversaries) and to create new statues that enable us to rapidly close risk exposure.

- Related to the previous point, we need to update Critical Infrastructure Partnership Advisory Council (CIPAC) authorities to incentivize the private sector to do more. Where these incentives do not suffice, dictate rules of security and safety to protect commercial critical infrastructure and make it more resilient. Exercise business and government continuity together.

Proposed Role for the House Foreign Affairs Committee.

The Committee should have a critical role in this subject area by first requiring a comprehensive review of the **USG International Strategy for Cyberspace** – what has been the result of actions taken thus far, what's not been done, and why. This will require the Administration to provide measures of effectiveness for the strategy. The Committee should ensure implementation measures address the worsening threat environment since the strategy was published in 2011.

Secondly, the Committee should ensure the Administration leads the rapid build-out of international public-private sector partnerships as an integral component of an effective deterrence strategy. In doing so, the State Department should be required to provide regular updates to the Committee on implementation status and to highlight to this committee any impediments to full implementation by the end of 2016. Further to this end, the Committee should work with the State Department to acquire authorities and/or resources to overcome impediments to strategy implementation.

Complementing and helping to enable the Administration's efforts on the international stage, the Committee should solicit regular updates from US-based Multinational Corporations on what else should be done to further US national interest in working with foreign nations to create an open, interoperable, secure and reliable cyberspace environment. This should include obtaining industry perspective on the effectiveness of current and proposed amendments to international trade and arms control agreements, such as the Wassenaar Arrangement on Export Controls for Conventional Arms and Dual-Use Goods and Technologies.

Finally, the Committee should set up a "table top" exercise that would help members to better understand different conflict scenarios which would involve cyberspace capabilities and highlight the role the Committee has in establishing mechanisms for prevention and response.

Thank you again for the opportunity to share these thoughts. I stand ready to help the Committee as we seek to better protect and grow our nation.

Mr. SALMON. Well, we will now begin member questions.

Last week President Xi Jinping visited the United States. Among other things, they came to an agreement on economic espionage, cyber espionage that neither country's government will conduct or knowingly support cyber-enabled theft of intellectual property with the intent of providing competitive advantages to companies or commercial sectors.

To me, the wording is vague and it gives both the U.S. and the Chinese side substantial room for interpretation.

Tell me, Dr. Lewis, does this agreement actually mean anything? Why do you believe President Obama chose to forego any public discussion of the grievous economic and security losses from China's previous attacks? And given that China believes that economic security is a national security imperative, do you predict whether China will actually substantially decrease or cease cyber theft in this realm?

Mr. LEWIS. Well, I would agree with you. Thank you for the question.

By the way, the very first time I ever testified 15 years ago was in front of this committee. I couldn't sleep the night before, I sweat through my shirt, and I stuttered. So it is a lot more fun being here as a private citizen.

Mr. CONNOLLY. Dr. Lewis, I have the same problem.

Mr. LEWIS. Yeah.

Mr. SALMON. Just stay awake for the answers, and we will be all right.

Mr. LEWIS. That is my advice.

It is a significant step forward, because for the first time a Chinese leader has addressed the issue of commercial espionage, and in the past, the Chinese have stoutly denied in public that they have any concern with this activity. In private, they have made the argument that for them commercial espionage is a national security issue, and so therefore they are legitimate in that kind of espionage.

In talking to administration officials, they know there is wiggle room in the language. They have told me they will be watching it closely to see how well the Chinese live up to their commitments. It is not an on/off switch. This is very difficult for Xi, in particular because the PLA, which is our primary actor, makes money. This is a source of extracurricular income for them, and they are not going to be happy giving it up.

But we can now count to a degree the number of economic espionage incidents that occur in the U.S., FBI and NSA can count them, and so that means if the Chinese live up to their agreement, the numbers should start to go down; if it stays the same or it goes up, we know they are not. And what I was told by, again, administration officials is sanctions are still on the table. They realize they may have to take action.

Mr. SALMON. Mr. Butler, despite affirmations and reassurances, we should still be prepared for malicious cyber incidents, correct?

Mr. BUTLER. [Nonverbal response.]

Mr. SALMON. With your prior military and government service and current private sector experience, what do you think our priorities should be in contingency planning for these attacks or for continued cyber espionage that targets our military and economic assets?

And lastly, for anyone on the panel after you address that question, if this government—or excuse me—if this agreement doesn't live up to its word, what should the U.S. Government do besides maybe sanctions? Are there other opportunities to escalate the severity of the issue? So what are some of the other options? Mr. Butler.

Mr. BUTLER. Thank you, Congressman Salmon. I think our priority is to get our own house in order here. We need to improve our defenses first and foremost. We can't go through another type of breach like we have seen of the magnitude and severity of the OPM breach. So finding ways to, what I would say, create cyber hygiene and doing that quickly will help us in a significant way. I think beyond that, it is now thinking through resiliency within the critical infrastructure. As a foundational piece, I think we need to continue to improve in our deterrence by denial activities.

At the same time, we need to think through how to establish norms much faster and find ways to enforce those norms. Again, I think one aspect of that is what I was discussing earlier, by bringing the private sector into the discussion to help us with understanding their perspective and looking at ways that we can tie together continuity of government and continuity of business-type activity.

Beyond that, and in terms of other options, we need to make sure that we not only speak about the potential for creating cost on the part of an adversary, but be able to show that. And that needs to be certainly in the demonstration of force, things like economic sanctions, but it is also showing the ability to be able to operate in spite of attacks. And so finding ways to work across the spectrum of those options, I think, is absolutely critical.

When we talk about deterrence today, it is cross-domain, it is the idea of using economic sanctions, potentially some other tools in the economic inventory that take us from beyond OFAC work into looking at ways that we could restrict travel of individuals into our country based on, you know, wrongful acts that are being prosecuted. It is certainly building the capability through our law enforcement activities and finding ways to not only name and shame, but to continue to work with entities like Interpol to help us with taking down illegal activity around the world. It is working to continue to grow the cyber mission forces that we have laid out in the defense cyber strategy. So I think it is a multi-faceted strategy, it is cross-domain deterrence.

Ms. LOTRIONTE. If I can add something to that. I think that with this agreement, it would be very good if the United States had a plan in place already for, one, how they are going to verify this. So, optimally right now, we would have measures in place and sensors in place that we would be able to basically approach the Chinese, and we would have to determine now which forum we would want to approach them in when and if they cheat in this agreement. Once that happens, though, I think we have to have, as Bob said, a cross-domain strategy.

And I would activate all those elements at once, meaning I would use law enforcement tools; I would start prosecuting those that are violating our domestic law; I would pull out all the options on sanctions, whether it is financial or others; I would also look at the WTO; and I would start bringing immediately—I would have the USTR ready to bring charges or claims against China for violations in the TRIPS agreement; and, of course, less spoken of publicly, I would have our intelligence organizations actively prepared to do counterintelligence and, in the more covert world, things to counter their actions.

So, I think we need to have that plan now and assume the worst, assume that they will cheat, so the minute they do, we have every avenue of the U.S. Government prepared to take action.

Mr. LEWIS. Just to build on that quickly, there was an intense debate within the administration on how to respond to the OPM hack, and sanctions were the middle course. Some people wanted to do more aggressive things, some people didn't want to do anything. So I think that the Chinese got the message that we were mad about this and would take action.

And in the future, to both strengthen deterrence and make sure there is compliance with the agreement, we probably will need to think about possible punitive actions, whether that is publishing financial data, leaking financial data on Chinese leaders, or erasing data on their servers, sanctions, indictments. There are a range of tools, but we will probably have to use them.

Chairman ROYCE [presiding]. We are going to go now to our ranking member, Mr. Eliot Engel.

Mr. ENGEL. Thank you, Mr. Chairman.

As your testimony shows, the international community has not yet formed a consensus on how to reduce cyber conflict. For example, some of our adversaries in cyberspace have advocated for an arms control approach, while America is focused on establishing global norms and confidence-building measures.

So let me ask Dr. Lewis and Mr. Butler, what do you see as the greatest factors motivating countries to support one approach over the other, and what are the most significant barriers to fostering a greater international consensus? Why don't we start with you, Dr. Lewis.

Mr. LEWIS. Thank you for the question.

One of the things that is interesting is that while there is a wide disparity of views on what we should do, all countries are afraid of cyber war, and this is from the biggest to the smallest, and many of them fear Cyber Command quite a bit. And I always wonder, should I tell them the truth or should I let them continue to believe that we are omnipotent, but that is the impression, and so it is that shared fear that drives the negotiation.

The dilemmas with a traditional arms control approach, which is the preferred Russian approach, is, it is difficult to define what is a cyber arm. They clearly would like to include information in that category. The Russians talked about information weapons, which doesn't make any sense, right, but they would like to control information, and they have supporters in the world.

So the treaty approach has verification problems, it has definition problems, and that is why the U.S. decided to go after norms of state behavior. You have to think about how you would verify compliance with norms and you have to think about penalties if norms aren't followed, but the arms control approach has just not been that useful because of its sort of structural problems that we face.

Mr. ENGEL. Thank you.

Mr. Butler.

Mr. BUTLER. Yes, Congressman Engel. I think the incentives and the factors for driving people into this discussion exist. Really everyone is affected by some type of malware or maliciousness that is going on in cyberspace, whether it is China, Russia, Iran, North Korea, our allies are affected, and so there is an incentive to come to the table and discuss. The challenge, as Jim indicated, is there is fear. There are also problems with taxonomy. We have different doctrines in terms of what is in cyberspace, and what is not in cyberspace, including these physical and logical structures.

We also are challenged with regards to understanding our overall objectives as we come to the table. As we look at, for instance, you know, the United States, we are trying to create an open and secure environment that allows for a global transaction platform and national security. Many countries see the benefits in that, but they see it as a U.S.-defined environment, and so going to multi-stakeholder types of venues actually helps us, the government group of experts, for instance.

And, finally, I would say that one of the other barriers is getting folks involved in the global economic system. And here is where the private sector again comes into play. I think it is important for nations, whether they are, you know, very, very developed or underdeveloped, to see where we are heading and helping folks to begin to see the value of being on the Internet.

There is this aspect of fear that not only comes from cyber war for high-end states, but as we think about some of the underdeveloped countries of the world not understanding exactly where we are going in terms of an interconnected society.

Mr. ENGEL. Thank you.

Dr. Lotrionte, let me throw a double-edged question at you. As international conflict increasingly moves into cyberspace, we need to be prepared for situations in which our military engages in hostilities overseas without deploying troops outside the United States. So in your opinion, would such activities trigger the congressional oversight and authorization requirements of the War Powers Resolution, and what steps should Congress take to ensure that cyber activities of the U.S. military fall within these oversight and authorization requirements?

And let me also add, as the United States works to develop global norms and customary international law governing cyber conflict, what legal clarifications are needed to ensure that we are able to prevent and respond to cyber threats by terrorist groups and other nonstate actors?

Ms. LOTRIONTE. Okay. Thank you for the two-part question.

First on your question with respect to the applicability of the War Powers Resolution, so as it is today, the language of that statute today, for most of the cyber activities that one could anticipate or think of where the U.S. would be conducting these activities abroad without soldiers engaged abroad, my position on that in the current state of the language is it is not applicable, meaning that if you look at the words within that statute, there could be a whole scope of cyber activities that would not trigger. So, if the President is honestly looking at that statute and trying to fulfill his reporting and consulting requirements, there are a lot of activities that would not be triggered.

There are two elements of that resolution that bring me to that reason. The two triggering elements for reporting are the words "armed forces" and "hostilities." And when you are talking about, not just cyber, but other emerging technologies, even drones, nanotechnology, there is a slew of new technologies in which this resolution is wholly inadequate in terms of covering.

But particularly with cyber, when you are talking about armed forces, that language needs to be expanded if you would like to cover and trigger that consulting and reporting requirement from the executive branch. As well as the phraseology with respect to hostilities, that has to also be expanded.

So, you know, for instance on the armed forces, it is not so much armed forces will be involved overseas necessarily when you are talking about the use of cyber tools by the President, but you need to use the language that would be suitable for that statute would be something to the effect of adding capabilities, language about capabilities, oriented provisions or supplies.

And as far as the phrase in the statute on hostilities, I would expand that language and not just leave it as it is today, but expand it to include it is not only engaging in hostilities, but it is also potentially the violation of the sovereignty of another nation that may trigger it.

Now, this, of course, would take some consultation, but if you ask me the original intent of that statute, if we wanted that original intent to consist today and you want the reporting and consulting that was envisioned for the legislative branch in the war-making process with the President, that is what I would say would need to be changed.

That was the first one. Would you like me to go on to the second question you had or——

Chairman ROYCE. Should we do that in writing?

Mr. ENGEL. I guess we can do that in writing.

Ms. LOTRIONTE. Okay.

Mr. ENGEL. Thank you.

Chairman ROYCE. Yeah. Thank you.

Let me ask a quick question to Dr. Lewis. We had the cyber attack on Turkey's electric grid. That was on March 31 of 2015. That was a 12-hour power outage, affected 40 million people in Turkey. You had the Iran cyber attack against American companies and the 2012 cyber attack on Saudi Arabia's oil conglomerate that destroyed the data on tens of thousands of computers.

So the question I have is what impact could the administration's lifting of sanctions on Iran have on Iran's cyber capabilities going forward?

Mr. LEWIS. It is a very good question and one that I think people, particularly in the financial sector, have been paying close attention to. The theory that most folks had was that Iran would be on its best behavior while the nuclear deal was being negotiated.

Chairman ROYCE. But they were hacking during the——they were doing the attacks during the deal.

Mr. LEWIS. Well, they weren't doing it as much as they were doing it against U.S. banks. They toned back a little bit. And the question is once this is completed, will they resume their activity, and so I think that is something that we are all watching.

My assumption is that Iran will be aggressive in the Persian Gulf. And the whole point of much of the discussion around the Sony episode——

Chairman ROYCE. Okay. I have got to stop you right there——

Mr. LEWIS. Okay.

Chairman ROYCE [continuing]. Because James Clapper says that Iran used cyber to attack U.S. military networks in December 2014. That would be in the middle of the Iranian nuclear negotiations. I don't know how you can present this thesis if they are in bad behavior in the middle of a negotiation where they are trying to get us to do what they want us to do, and now you say, well, now afterwards, after we have lost the leverage, they are going to change their behavior. And let me go to another question.

Mr. LEWIS. Oh, change their behavior for the worst.

Chairman ROYCE. Yeah.

Mr. LEWIS. This is not——one of the changes in the last few years has been significant improvement on Iran's attack capabilities.

Chairman ROYCE. Yeah.

Mr. LEWIS. So the concern is will they use them against the U.S.? And they used them against Sands.

Chairman ROYCE. Yeah.

Mr. LEWIS. You know, so——

Chairman ROYCE. Yeah. Well, very good. I appreciate that, Dr. Lewis.

I have got a question for Bob Butler. The DNI, our Director of National Intelligence, says he doesn't think that the agreement announced last week during the visit of President Xi is going to impact the bottom line in how China attempts to access U.S. computer systems, including our intellectual property. I was going to see if you agree with that. How do you gauge that agreement? Is it going to affect the cyber conflict? Are they going to honor the agreement?

Mr. BUTLER. I think the proof is in the pudding. We are going to have to wait and see. We had an agreement on Friday. We have also had an informal announcement about the Chinese not being very happy with some of our positions on U.S. Internet policy since then. I think we need to see from a validation and verification standpoint with regards to the follow-through on this.

My sense is the wording is important. You know, there was no agreement, of course, on espionage writ large, specifically on commercial secrets and how that is interpreted. So I think we need to put in place immediately some type of validation and verification scheme that takes advantage of our national intelligence apparatus, but also capabilities that we have in the private sector to understand what exactly is changing and how it is changing as we go forward in time.

Chairman ROYCE. Let me ask a question of Dr. Lotrionte. Which U.S. Government agencies are responsible for addressing cyberwar-related threats and response and recovery efforts? Because the point I want to make is should the Department of Defense protect the cybersecurity of the U.S. homeland from significant cyber attacks? And is it really time for us to look at this just as, you know, during the second world war, we stood up the Air Force as a separate branch in order to give that responsibility, give that authority? Is it time to do something like that?

Ms. LOTRIONTE. So I think there are multiple agencies and departments that have underneath their legal mission or authority a role to play both in preventing, but also countering and responding.

First I would start with State Department, the significant role in the diplomacy. In order to have a form of deterrence, we need to have the establishment of some agreements, these norms, right, to make a link——

Chairman ROYCE. You know what, what I am going to ask you to do, as an attorney, you have a great background in this: Could you delineate that in writing for me, because I am about to be out of time and I wanted to ask Bob Butler one more question?

If a cyber attack took down our financial system or took down the electrical grid, would the United States consider it a use of force, and if so, how would we determine who to strike back and who to strike against?

And, Dr. Lotrionte, I am going to ask you that too, but, Bob?

Mr. BUTLER. Sure. Mr. Chairman, certainly from the vantage point of taking down life safety systems, the grid, water treatment systems, and looking at our financial services, I think that would be of serious consequence. We are planning, from a DOD standpoint, national teams to support that.

In terms of figuring it out, you know, I think we have to understand what the "roll-up" is to cyber conflict, and maybe I will just take 30 seconds here to explain how that takes place.

I mean, initially we see reconnaissance activity, right? We see people scanning networks. We then see people crawling on networks. Then we see focused targeting of activity based on our knowledge—based on the adversary's knowledge from what they have done on reconnaissance and surveillance activities. Then potentially we see exploitation through malware that could lead to stealing things. It could also be an implant that basically positions someone for a further attack, whether it is disruptive or destructive.

We would need to find and "lay in" intelligence both on the national security side and with commercial sensors to help us understand what is "going on," on the network.

Chairman ROYCE. Well, okay. So here is what I am going to do. I am out of time, but——

Mr. BUTLER. Yes.

Chairman ROYCE [continuing]. If any of the three witnesses for the last two questions have some ideas here in terms of attribution techniques and how we could follow up on that, because that is what you are getting to, that would be helpful to the committee.

We now go to Karen Bass of California.

Ms. BASS. Thank you, Mr. Chair.

In listening to your testimony, I wanted to know if either one of you, you know, out of the three could give me examples of where you think other countries are doing a good job in terms of cybersecurity, and maybe there are some lessons that we can learn from there.

And then I believe it was you, Mr. Butler, that were talking about the consequences and maybe imposing sanctions on individuals. But then, how do we address it when a lot of this is state run?

And then finally, sorry to load up all my questions, but when I think of some of the major terrorist groups that we are dealing with, whether it is Al Qaeda or ISIS, or the Taliban, what level of involvement do they have in cyber attacks?

Mr. LEWIS. I will start. Let me come back briefly to the earlier question, though, which is to if you want to get the Iranians to change how they think about this, you don't want to take a passive approach, and that has been one of our problems——

Ms. BASS. Are you——

Mr. LEWIS [continuing]. One of our problems in cybersecurity. We need to make credible threats and we need to have countries believe that we will respond with some punitive action.

Not a lot of people are doing a good job on this. The Israelis have done a good job, but not perfect. The Russians have done a good job, the French, and to some extent the British. That might be it in the world. We do okay, but one of the things we need to do is make people believe that if they hack us, there will be punishment, and that is maybe the most important thing we can do.

Ms. BASS. And are any of our intelligence agencies cooperating or taking lessons and implementing practices from the countries you just mentioned?

Mr. LEWIS. We have really close relations with the British. We have okay relations with the Israelis and the French, good relations, but not as close as the British. So there is an effort in the context of our alliances to build a collective defense.

Ms. BASS. Thank you.

Mr. BUTLER. Let me go to your first question with regards to states that are doing good work in the area of cybersecurity. I think the U.S. model and allied models continue to grow. And when I look at really good work going on around the globe. I think of the partnerships that we have in place.

So, if I look at the Japanese Computer Emergency Response Team, which is really the APAC Computer Emergency Response Team, they have taken lessons learned from what we have done and others, and are really doing a pretty good job in tracking advanced persistent threats.

When I think about, for instance, what are we doing on the global transaction platform, the Financial Services-ISAC, or Information Sharing and Analysis Center, has broadened their approach to where they are now looking globally as opposed to just within the country.

There is a new activity that has stood up in Singapore that is an extension of Interpol—Global Center for Innovation. Here, a model that we, I think, pioneered, maybe some others were involved in terms of botnet takedowns, proactive botnet ''takedowns,'' is being worked on on a global basis.

So I think both on the proactive/prevention side as well as on the prevent, or on the response side, there are models that we can look at. And, again, we have been involved with helping others in that area, but we can also learn from that as well.

In terms of sanction enforcements, I think, again, it is a combination of trust and verify. So there are different economic and trade remedies that could be employed. We need to look at the impact as best we know it would have on the nation-state, and then we need to think through the enforcement, the verification mechanism, and certainly intelligence is involved in there, but we could also ensure validation through a partner working in conjunction with us against that potential adversary.

In terms of looking at the terrorist issue, deterrence is different. I like to talk about tailored deterrence against nation-states, a nation-state, and what is required to deter that particular actor. A lot of the things we have been talking about lately really are focused on determined resource nation-states as opposed to terrorist groups.

And in this space, we need to think hard about, you know, for instance, in ISIS, that is growing in social media campaigns and recruiting and creating challenges for us. How do we deter those kinds of actors and how do we deter actors that are really where we don't know a lot about their doctrine?

Ms. BASS. Thank you. I appreciate it.

Dr. Lotrionte?

Ms. LOTRIONTE. In terms of other countries working well on the cybersecurity front, I would put in a word for the Brits in terms of what I have seen they do. Now, a lot in the awareness area and also working with their universities. They have less than we do in this country, but they have done a lot of good work, the government has, in reaching out and coordinating to understand what resources on that, the higher education level, and putting in R&D as well.

I think they are not better than us, but they have followed our lead in most of the ways that we have communicated with the private sector. I think they also are working on getting better at that, sending out warnings to their companies about the nature of the threat.

But I would say in general, and this is not always the case, I think the U.S. is the lead in this, and the Europeans, I have heard the Europeans say that. And I have often had, whether it is the Japanese or the Germans or other East Asian countries, when they come into town, the officials are coming into town and going to the State Department, they often come to me and they have asked me, talk to me about how the U.S. is handling and doing their cybersecurity work. And they are looking to us for good examples, for models. So I think that might be my general sense.

On the sanctions, over the years watching how under international law targeted sanctions, while slow in terms of their effectiveness, can ultimately be effective. I think you can do very targeted, smart sanctions against individuals. You know, I personally like the thought of freezing assets. When people lose their money and they no longer can get their money, you usually see some effect.

Ms. BASS. Thank you.

Ms. LOTRIONTE. And terrorist groups are also definitely, as Bob has already said, a consideration we have to deal with.

Ms. BASS. Thank you very much.

Chairman ROYCE. We go now to Mr. Dana Rohrabacher of California.

Mr. ROHRABACHER. Thank you very much, Mr. Chairman.

I guess we are talking about a number of approaches to this sort of new subject. I don't think anybody talked about this 10, 20 years ago. And what you just said when we were talking about a retaliation, I was thinking in terms of retaliation versus sanctions.

Would it not be better to try to set up a system where we are not offering some sort of economic sanction, but instead if we catch you and your people, how do you say, disturbing our system, our economic system in some way or our weapons systems, that we will just retaliate against your systems? That the Chinese banks will have to experience some problems if people keep hacking into our banks? Isn't that what—wouldn't that be more effective than telling the Chinese Government, you are going to not be able to deliver anymore widgets over here that you have manufactured?

Ms. LOTRIONTE. I can——

Mr. ROHRABACHER. And we will ask our whole panel that. Go right ahead.

Ms. LOTRIONTE. I can say something about the law, at least international law. Well, first, absolutely correct: 10 years ago we weren't dealing with the level of threats, and therefore, it wasn't really a conversation about talking about responses, right, and how to react to this. But since then, luckily, a lot of people have given a lot of their time internationally to think about the rules that we had and have today, can we actually use them effectively to actually respond in a pretty effective and meaningful way?

And, yes, it is sometimes economic, you try to use the, if you will, less escalatory means to resolve this dispute, right, whatever it is, and the law actually requires that. But at times you will need to actually go to the higher level of the spectrum and maybe use force.

So most of what my written statement for the record, that I have given you, but also I tried to summarize it really quickly was that is why I put most emphasis on really looking at some key terminology that we have all accepted under international law, use of force in armed attack, and come to agreement on what those terms mean. Why is that important? Well, it is because then we will all know where the line is.

Mr. ROHRABACHER. Right. I understand that part of your testimony.

Ms. LOTRIONTE. And I think you can use force.

Mr. ROHRABACHER. I think the gentleman would like to comment as well.

Mr. LEWIS. Sure. Thank you, Congressman.

So we talked earlier about a deterrence deficit. People don't believe that the U.S. will take action in response——

Mr. ROHRABACHER. Right.

Mr. LEWIS [continuing]. To these cyber things, and so we——

Mr. ROHRABACHER. There is no deterrent unless there is a capability of retaliating.

Mr. LEWIS. Well, we have the capability, it is people don't think we will do it. And so one of the most important things we could do is think, how do we persuade the people like the Irans, the Chinas, the Russias that we would retaliate for some kind of cyber action. And many of us are coming to the belief that——

Mr. ROHRABACHER. Give me——

Mr. LEWIS [continuing]. We might have to do it once.

Mr. ROHRABACHER. Give me an example of when you say, we will retaliate, what that would mean.

Mr. LEWIS. You have a range of options. You could, for example, with OPM, you could have erased data on some of the Chinese computer networks that held the OPM data. That wouldn't have taken it away. It is gone forever. But it would have sent a signal. You could leak financial data on Chinese leadership. You could interfere with the power grid. There is a whole range of things we could do. But I think the fear is until we do something, and it might be sanctions, until we show some reaction, people won't take our threats seriously.

Mr. ROHRABACHER. Mr. Butler, do you want to——

Mr. BUTLER. I think it is important to look at who we are trying to deter. So in China, for instance, if you go back and just look at August and the Shanghai Exchange, I mean, something that would hurt would be to impact, you know, them economically. They are trying to be part of a global economic system——

Mr. ROHRABACHER. Give me an example of what you think we would—if China has these assets that they are now building that will hurt us, what would we do with our capabilities to retaliate against a Chinese, well, they already are, apparently, breaking into our banking system, et cetera.

Mr. BUTLER. If we could impact them adversely in an economic way, I think that will have a significant impact on it. I mean more and more, I see people like Jack Ma of Alibaba, Huawei, and ZTE driving into the global economic system, and needing business outside of China. And they have influence in China.

On the flip side of it, we have organizations, U.S.-based multinationals that have relationships in China and actually have Chinese clients. We should be taking advantage of that to shape the environment to our advantage, as opposed to waiting for something and then reacting.

Mr. ROHRABACHER. I think this is a very fruitful discussion, but only probably the first one that we should have on this issue. And let me note that—let me ask this. When the chairman mentioned the cyber attack that may have taken place with the Iranians against some of our naval vessels, could that have been in retaliation for, perhaps, an Israeli attack on their reactors?

Mr. LEWIS. I don't know in that particular case. In other cases, there probably has been some retaliation because of attacks attributed to Israel. So the Kharg Island incident where the Iranian oil——

Mr. ROHRABACHER. We are going to have to make sure that we establish, and this hearing is the first step toward getting an honest discussion of this, so I thank the chairman for scheduling this hearing because we are going to need to know how to verify that there has been an attack, verify who the attack is from. We are going to determine what type of protection that we can have that will nullify or at least protect us against these attacks, what type of systems we need.

And then we need to discuss if there are attacks like this, what type of retaliation, what are our options of retaliation. And as we heard earlier, even the wording as to what will, what will justify a type of retaliation, just the wording of it, we haven't even determined that yet.

Mr. LEWIS. That is a really important——

Chairman ROYCE. And maybe, Doctor, we can respond to that in writing.

We are going to go to Alan Lowenthal from California.

Mr. LOWENTHAL. Thank you, Mr. Chair. And I want to thank the panelists. I mean, this is something that I am just learning myself and I find it fascinating but I certainly don't consider myself an expert in any way.

I would like to return now when we are dealing with cybersecurity, rather than the focus on where the attacks come from on our own infrastructure and how much we are doing to protect ourselves and our infrastructure. I believe that the President has issued an Executive order pledging, I think it was 13636, to improve our infrastructure, critical infrastructure in terms of cybersecurity.

I would like to know what significant security developments have resulted from that Executive order. Has it been effective? How much of our own critical infrastructure is vulnerable? And what are we doing about our own infrastructure to understand the vulnerabilities that we face today? Anybody want to jump in? Again, to my edification. It may be common knowledge to everyone else but it certainly isn't to me.

Mr. BUTLER. I think it is a great question. With the Executive order and actually prior to the Executive order, certainty our life/safety systems sectors have been taking action. They have been incentivized through the government to take more action.

Again, I will just start with financial services and our banks and related financial service activities, they have been practicing, you know, in terms of incident response for some time. They have been doing a lot of information sharing. They have gone beyond information sharing into joint solutioning. They have helped to develop automated ways of information sharing to find new standards, and they have taken that globally.

When I look at what is going on in the energy world, we have work to do. Our energy grid is a challenge. And based on the regulatory nature of how FERC and NERC work to support different utilities, co-ops, and consortiums. We need to find ways to actually not only create incentives but work through standards and get the grid to a point where it is a lot more resilient than it is today. As we build that new infrastructure.

Mr. LOWENTHAL. Have we not looked at these issues over time? Is that really, we did we not understand the vulnerabilities to our private sector and allowed them to develop without even questioning some of these issues? And is that true in terms of our own, say, Department of Defense which may have been more responsive to some of these issues earlier? I don't understand the difference between the private sector development and the public sector development, the defense development.

Mr. BUTLER. In the Department of Defense, we have been working on the whole issue of cyberspace and operating effectively in cyberspace for years. We have continued to try to ramp up and improve our defenses as we work through concepts for growing cyberspace as an operational domain in conflict and warfare.

From the private sector perspective, there has been different levels of understanding and knowledge, primarily driven by business motives. And so the financial services, even before the 2012/2013 attacks, the distributed denial-of-service attacks, were moving in a very accelerated direction to make themselves more resilient on a global transaction platform.

I would say oil and natural gas is getting there, but they are late to the game. And they are working hard to catch up. They have to work through different kinds of upstream and downstream activities to kind of ensure that people understand at all levels within an organization, to include their supply chain, what is at stake. Certainly Saudi Aramco woke them up to that.

On the grid side, in California, we have seen the physical attacks up in Menlo Park and the Metcalf substation. Since those physical attacks, there has been lots of educational outreach in terms of ensuring utilities in California and elsewhere are moving in that direction. The challenge is rate structures. It costs to build security.

And one of the issues that I am constantly faced with on the private sector side is how do I generate a return on investment as I build into security? What the President has done and the administration has done is opening up a new dialogue that allows us to drive more into incentivizing the private sector through threat sharing, ability of using CIPAC, Critical Infrastructure Partnership Advisory Council, authorities to get limited liability protections, collaborate with government and others that are ahead in this game, and to drive us to a new level so all boats rise together from the country's standpoint. But it is taking time.

Mr. LEWIS. We started talking about this in 1998. In fact, we started talking about this in 1996. So it has been a slow progress. But banks, telecommunications companies, and defense industrial companies are generally at the top of the league, they are the best. Electrical grid it is a very mixed performance. Some companies do good, some don't.

One thing to watch is the new industry. So everyone knows your car is slowly becoming a rolling computer. So the auto industries, the airplane industries, they are beginning to focus on cybersecurity. But it varies from sector to sector. And we haven't found a good way to change that.

Mr. LOWENTHAL. Thank you, Mr. Chairman.

Chairman ROYCE. Thank you. We go to Mr. Randy Weber.

Mr. WEBER. Thank you. Mr. Butler, what is the price, how high of a price is water if you can't get it? What price would you pay?

Mr. BUTLER. I think it is needed for life.

Mr. WEBER. Yes. Whatever it is——

Mr. BUTLER [continuing]. Price on it.

Mr. WEBER. I am fascinated by the exchange with you and Mr. Lowenthal about the infrastructure, for example. And the thought occurs to me on energy, electricity, we have got to have it.

Mr. BUTLER. Right.

Mr. WEBER. We absolutely have to have it. So maybe a redundant system, one that is connected, both of them connected to the grid, and I know the price, you mentioned rates would be important, I get that. But there is people who have to have dialysis or police departments have to run, or military, it is a security and it is a life issue in a lot of ways. So maybe the answer to that is a redundant setup where you have two power plants side by side, I know, cost is a factor, one that is controlled, you know, through the Internet, if you will.

And I have pipelines all over the State of Texas. And they actually can control the entire pipeline across the country from their control room. So maybe that is the answer. Maybe you have a standalone unit that is not connected to the Internet so none of our enemies can shut it down. But yet it can snap on line in just a matter of seconds or minutes more appropriately. So interesting discussion. Dr. Lewis, you said that advanced cyber capability, in your comments there was five countries, U.S., U.K., Russia, China, and Israel. Define advanced cyber capability.

Mr. LEWIS. The usual way to look at it is they could cause physical destruction. They could cause the kind of disruption in services that you were talking about. They could turn off electrical plants.

Mr. WEBER. Is it safe to say that they have, for lack of a better term, a military officer or probably a 12-year-old kid in a computer room, that can hack—that is what they do, that is their job?

Mr. LEWIS. The bad news is the countries that don't like us, including Iran, Russia, and China, have probed our critical infrastructure and have looked for vulnerabilities and are prepared to turn it off if necessary.

Mr. WEBER. Okay. What is the percentage of their success? Mr. Butler, you mentioned earlier they are watching people monitor the grid. Would you say that of those people who are trying to attack us, are they 1 percent successful, 10 percent successful?

Mr. LEWIS. My guess would be, I don't know what Bob thinks, it would be closer to 100 percent.

Mr. WEBER. Well, that is encouraging. And you said Russia and China, you ought to be putting sanctions on it. Is a reverse hacking, are we able to reverse hack them? Now, somebody mentioned, you know, maybe it was Dr. Lotrionte? Is that how you say that? Said releasing the personal financial information of Chinese leaders? Are you advocating that we have a department in our military, if you will, that actually does that, hacks to get back at them and then, is that what you are saying?

Mr. LEWIS. One of the problems in this whole thing is we have taken kind of a passive approach. We have taken a technical approach. We have focused on making our defenses strong which you could call it a Maginot Line approach. We have to find ways——

Mr. WEBER. How did that work with the French by the way?

Mr. LEWIS. We don't want to be on the same path.

Mr. WEBER. You think?

Mr. LEWIS. I think we need to find ways to demonstrate to countries that we will not put up with this.

Mr. WEBER. So, Dr. Lotrionte, am I saying that right?

Ms. LOTRIONTE. You are.

Mr. WEBER. Okay. And you said in 2005 was really the first appearance of was it a cyber crime, was that international legislation? I missed that. That got by me. Do you remember?

Ms. LOTRIONTE. Was that the 2008, the armed conflict that I was mentioning?

Mr. WEBER. That is what it was. Thank you.

Ms. LOTRIONTE. I wanted to set it up to say we are starting to see the cyber tools and operations be used within armed conflicts. And they are continuing. But first for state level it was 2008 in Georgia and Russia.

Mr. WEBER. I am surprised that it took that long, quite frankly. And then, Dr. Lewis, you said the Israelis did a good job on responding. What does that look like?

Mr. LEWIS. They have an advantage because they are a small country. And one of the things that they have is they use their military to identify talent. So they recruit kids out of high school.

Mr. WEBER. That is that set, like I was talking about in China, they have got a group of people that that is their attack, that is their platoon or whatever you want to call it. That is their job.

Mr. LEWIS. The Israelis are under attack probably every week by Hezbollah, very low level attacks, and probably by Iran, by the Syrian Electronic Army.

Mr. WEBER. Well, we are too I mean not necessarily by those entities but others.

Mr. LEWIS. They are a lot smaller. And so they don't have what you would call strategic depth. So they get a lot of practice. People are a little more afraid of attacking us. But we need to make them more afraid.

Mr. WEBER. Okay. All right. Thank you, Mr. Chairman. I yield back.

Chairman ROYCE. We go now to Mr. Ted Poe of Texas.

Mr. POE. Thank you, Mr. Chairman. The cyber attack on Sony Pictures Entertainment by North Korea, in your opinion, Dr. Lewis, is that an act of terrorism?

Mr. LEWIS. Yeah, so it is one of these things that falls in this gray area because they did disrupt Sony Pictures, they leaked damaging materials, they put out emails. It was a coercive act, right? Now, whether you call that terrorism or not, I would call it coercion. The North Koreans probably intended it to terrify Sony. So they were doing this intentionally to punish Sony for that movie.

Mr. POE. North Korea used to be on the State Sponsors of Terrorism List. They are off. Do you think we should reconsider that, Dr. Lewis? Just your opinion.

Mr. LEWIS. Sure. No, I don't. Because it is, what influences how countries think about this doesn't have to do with sanctions that are external to that or terrorism lists that are external to that. We need to think about things that directly apply to cybersecurity. And that is where the committee might want to do some work. Putting them back on the list or taking them off, it is not going to affect their behavior. We need to do things that are more direct.

Mr. POE. Because their behavior is bad.

Mr. LEWIS. Yes. Oh, yeah.

Mr. POE. Let me ask the other two witnesses, same question, do you think it is an act of terrorism? And if you think it is, should they be put back on the list? Just your opinion. Both of you. All three witnesses.

Mr. BUTLER. I rarely disagree with Jim. I think we need to spend more time thinking about what the North Koreans are really trying to do here. They are building a cyber capability. And they did achieve their desired effect in really terrorizing a large entertainment firm. Where is that going to go? And so I think, I wouldn't rule it out in terms of putting them back on an established terrorist list. But I think we need to spend more time understanding where they are growing with their capabilities, as well as intent.

Ms. LOTRIONTE. If I took a very legalistic approach to it, under international law, I would call that not an act of terrorism but a violation of the norm of non-intervention under international law which is——

Mr. POE. Wait a minute. Wait a minute. Wait a minute. What did you just say?

Ms. LOTRIONTE. Not to get in the weeds, but the norm of non-invention under international law which is——

Mr. POE. The norm of non-intervention under international law.

Ms. LOTRIONTE. It is what Lewis described as coercive. It is by definition coercive interference when you are basically bleeding or forcing a state to give up one of its fundamental rights under international law. And that typically is seen as political elections. But also it can be the freedom of speech. So this was illegal, in my view, under international law. It was a violation of the norm of non-intervention but not terrorism.

Mr. POE. Okay. And just following up on that, the Sony situation, any consequences for that attack? Were there any consequences on the North Koreans for doing what they did?

Ms. LOTRIONTE. As a policy matter——

Mr. POE. Did somebody call them to the principal's office? Were they retaliated against? Did we hack into their system? I mean, was there any type of response to that act by Sony? I mean by——

Mr. LEWIS. I think they were scared. So one of the things that has come up repeatedly in the questioning is our ability to attribute the source of an attack. And about 8 years ago, DOD started to work really hard with a lot of money in—to be able to figure out who is doing the hacking. And I think the North Koreans were shocked that we were able to tell so quickly that it was them. And that scared them.

Five years ago, they did another attack on U.S. facilities, not as bad. We never were quite sure. This time we knew it was them. We could take pictures of the guys doing it. Right. So it is that improved attribution capability that scared them.

Ms. LOTRIONTE. So to answer that question, was there a response or retaliation, what was publicly, at least, available to know, it does not appear that the U.S. took a public move in response, retaliation.

Now, I would hope or assume that our intelligence organizations have responded to that. And under international law, a countermeasure to a violation of a norm of non-intervention is appropriate and legal. So if we have legal authority to take a countermeasure, it has to be non-forcible, I would think that would be in the baili-wick of the intelligence community to do that. And we might not see or talk about that publicly.

Mr. POE. Okay. I will yield back, Mr. Chairman.

Chairman ROYCE. Mr. Ted Yoho of Florida.

Mr. YOHO. Thank you, Mr. Chairman. And thank you for having this very important meeting. And I would propose or recommend, not recommend, I would ask that we build on this hearing to define what constitutes a cyber attack and when it is an act of war or an act of terror, and define systems that fall under that, whether it is our electrical system, military system, power systems, hospitals, and whether that is a certain amount of life lost, any life lost, or economic, a major economic catastrophe.

And, Dr. Lewis, you were saying we have known about this since 1996. That is 20 years. Twenty years and we still don't have a defi-nition or a policy. I think that is way too long. We have just dropped the ball on this. And who is watching the hen house? I mean, this is not acceptable.

Number one charge of America's Government, as we all know, is national security. This is a national security threat. And technology will continue to advance, become more complex in the future. And we are going to be more intertwined with that. And to not have those kind of policies in place is a shortfall of administrations, not just this one but of past ones. And this is something we need to get on right now. We should have been on it.

I am glad, I am sure there is a lot more going on behind the scenes than we hear about. I am sure it is like Jack Nicholson in that movie you can't stand, you can't tolerate the truth or you don't want to know it. And I think to ask you what constitutes an act of war or an act of terrorism, do we have a definition of that?

Ms. LOTRIONTE. So I will, one, I agree with you in terms of the amount of time it has taken to get to the point we are where we are actually talking about the specific definitions and norms I think has been too long. And it does remind me when I was in the intelligence community, the years leading up to 9/11. And it was like a good 15, 20 years it took people to understand what would be an armed attack under the law by non-state actors like terror-ists that would allow us to use force in response against them on somebody else's sovereign territory. And I think it took us too long.

So here we are in a different context, different types of threats, of course, but the same principles that need to be discussed and de-fined. So, really the focus of my whole point and my written state-ment was that we do need to get agreement on some very impor-tant terms with respect to international law and the use of force and armed conflict. Specifically, what is a use of force for purposes of Article 2(4) of the U.N. Charter. What is an armed attack for purposes of Article 5(1) of the U.N. Charter which allows a country to use forcible measures in response.

And so I think that we have had some laws that have developed at the U.N., for instance, with respect to non-state actors. After 9/11, the U.N. Security Council passed two very important resolutions which cleared up the law and said you can go and you can use force and retaliate against even non-state actors.

Mr. YOHO. That was U.S. law?

Ms. LOTRIONTE. Well, it is U.S. law.

Mr. YOHO. It is fine that the U.N. has that, but the U.S. needs to have our own definition so we don't need to go to the U.N. We are saying we need to put this out to the world that if you do this, this is our response.

And, Dr. Lewis, you were saying we need to have a credible response. Unfortunately, our Government right now has lost a lot of credibility. We draw red lines in disappearing ink. We call for regime change and deny it. I mean, we go on and on. Again, it is not just this administration. It is what America stands for.

We have got to be able to project credibility with a policy and be willing to back it up. And what, you know, what I would like to see is what is the appropriate response the U.S. should state it will do? Is it to retaliate and to put other countries on notice in the beginning and say this is what we are going to do? And is it an eye for an eye response as my colleague Dana Rohrabacher said? Or is it, you know, we are going to respond two or three or four times worse than whatever you did? What is your thoughts on that?

Mr. LEWIS. You touched on some key points. And Bob is being a little modest here, but DOD has actually done a good job of coming up with doctrine on offensive use, defensive use of cyber——

Mr. YOHO. I would like to see that. And I would like to build that. Because if somebody comes into my house uninvited, it is not going to be a nice response. You know, and that is what I feel they are doing here. They are invading our privacy. They are invading our sovereignty. And for us to not have a response stated and put people on notice I think is just such a shortfall. Mr. Butler?

Mr. BUTLER. Yes. Just building on the conversation, I mean we have levels of activity, exploitation, disruption, destruction. When we hit disruption and destruction, we have a problem. And that should signal to the national command authorities we need to take action.

The challenge inside this space is making sure we have the indications and warning before it happens. For instance, we need to have some signaling with regards to what is happening to our industrial control systems. If malware drops into our industrial control systems, that should be a signal that we should be thinking about taking action to counter, before something rises to another level and we actually get into aggression.

Mr. YOHO. All right. Let me ask you this. With North Korea attacking Sony, we have had people here saying it wasn't North Korea, it was China working through North Korea as a proxy. What do we do when another country, a nation-state, works through a proxy, maybe Hezbollah in the future, some terrorist organization, but we know it was directed by a nation-state? And if we don't have time, if I could get a response to that, I would love to hear that.

Ms. LOTRIONTE. Do you want me to just——

Mr. YOHO. Go ahead.

Ms. LOTRIONTE. So non-state actors as proxies for state's actions, right? Well, yes, we have authority. And it is under international law. And the U.S. could accept it to take action against the state who is, if you can attribute, if you can attribute the actions of the non-state actors to the state, you can use force and take it to the state, hold them responsible.

Ms. LEWIS. One place we get hung up on, and this is where the committee could help, is we get hung up on what is a proportional response. So there is a lot of debate, what is a proportional response to Sony? And that is where having some guidelines or some principles.

There is a second issue, though, which is the one you brought up which is maybe sometimes we don't want to be proportional in our response. And that would be useful to have guidelines on as well.

Mr. YOHO. Thank you. Thank you, Mr. Chairman, for the extra time.

Chairman ROYCE. Thank you. We will pursue that question. We will go to Mr. Brad Sherman of California.

Mr. SHERMAN. We don't play offense. China hacks. We don't talk about what tariff to put on all Chinese products in order to compensate ourselves for that. Not even allowed to talk about that in polite society. It is much easier for bureaucracies to say we want money for defense. Offense, oh my God, it is not politically correct.

The unique vulnerability of China, and to some extent Russia, is the incredible corruption. We have the capacity through cyber and other means to identify which princeling owns which chateaus. Dr. Lewis, do we have the capacity to find, document, and leak to the press the ill-gotten foreign assets of Chinese leaders and their children?

Mr. LEWIS. I believe we do, particularly because many of those assets are located in the United States.

Mr. SHERMAN. And if you are trying to embarrass a regime, there is, you know, entries on a Merrill Lynch form are interesting but—pictures of chateaus, mcmansions, et cetera, are more so.

Dr. L, to what extent do we play offense in the sense of not just gathering, traditional statecraft, spying on governments and feeding it into our intel operation? To what extent do we play offense beyond that?

Ms. LOTRIONTE. I certainly think we have the capability. I also think we have the authority, legal authority, particularly Cyber Command in its authority legislated by Congress gives it both defensive and offensive capability. Unfortunately, I think because of the nature of those——

Mr. SHERMAN. Could we, for example, steal Chinese proprietary company, corporate information and just either hand it to an American company, which would raise huge questions which company, or just publish it?

Ms. LOTRIONTE. If the U.S. Government——

Mr. SHERMAN. Yes.

Ms. LOTRIONTE [continuing]. Determined that they wanted as a matter of policy to conduct economic espionage, they could do it.

Mr. SHERMAN. And do we have the legal authority to then publish the results?

Ms. LOTRIONTE. Yes.

Mr. SHERMAN. Do we have the authority to give it to those companies that correctly choose which political party to donate to?

Ms. LOTRIONTE. Yes.

Mr. SHERMAN. You mean, we could leak it to one company and not another?

Ms. LOTRIONTE. Well, when we discuss the economic espionage part, I think that is a concern of agencies in the U.S. Government, would there be any liability in terms of choosing between companies that benefit. Well, you can solve that by actually having a framework for, similar to when you put out a bid for a contract. There are processes——

Mr. SHERMAN. You mean, we would announce that we had stolen secret technology to build printing presses and then have companies bid? That would be interesting.

Ms. LOTRIONTE. I think so too, sir.

Mr. SHERMAN. And you say we would have all the legal authority to do that? If we had a President that wanted to go in, steal some corporate—now, the problem we have here, what is asymmetrical is, we got a lot more intellectual property than they do. So that is, I don't want to get in a tit for tat steal intellectual property world. What I would rather do is get them to stop.

Mr. Butler, can you think of any other offensive cyber techniques that we could use that the Chinese and the Russians would find painful?

Mr. BUTLER. I think for the Chinese, and as I mentioned earlier, as they are trying to integrate into the global economic system. Anything that we could do that would impact their growth potential, Huawei, ZTE, Baidu, Alibaba, I think would have an impact. I think like you said, sir——

Mr. SHERMAN. But it is asymmetric. Alibaba might want access to the U.S. market. Google does want access to the Chinese market.

Mr. BUTLER. Right. Right.

Mr. SHERMAN. The easiest thing, of course, is just tariffs on their imported goods. And the asymmetrical way is to go after the corruption because, and I gather from this panel there are no legal obstacles to espionage designed to identify and prove ill-gotten gains held by Chinese leaders and their children, and leak that to the press, in both China and the United States. Mr. Lewis, do you see any legal bar to that?

Mr. LEWIS. No. I was just going to say that it would apply equally to Russia.

Mr. SHERMAN. Yes. I think, I think it would have less political impact in Russia, although that regime has to be a little shaky. I mean, China is trying to explain to its people why under their great leadership they may have to suffer with less than 7 percent growth. Putin has to explain a world of $44 a barrel oil which is a much more painful world. Doctor, do you have——

Ms. LOTRIONTE. I would just say, I think you wanted to reconfirm about the legality of it. Not only would that be legal, but in the past, as far as the first half of that scenario, doing it to them and leaking it, we have history outside of this cyber context that the intelligence community has done things like that before. So both legal under international law and under domestic law.

Mr. SHERMAN. Okay. And so we have in pre-cyber methodology obtained embarrassing information about the leaders and families of countries we are not entirely friendly with and leaked it to the press. Unless Mr. Butler has a comment, I yield back.

Chairman ROYCE. I want to thank our witnesses. There is one more favor that the panel could do for this committee if you would. Mr. Ted Yoho of Florida had two other questions that we would like to get your response in writing to if we could. Mr. Yoho, do you want to lay out those two questions?

Mr. YOHO. Yes, sir, Mr. Chairman. I appreciate it. The first one is what is your recommendation to help facilitate our Government working with private industry or, vice versa, industry working with our Government to prevent or alert each other about attacks. That is question number one.

The second one which is really two questions, are there any laws prohibiting us to follow through on these, you know, something prohibiting us. And I know we have got to go through the U.N. to be nice and all that. But, again, my concern is the sovereignty and the protection of the United States Government, and that law ought to trump everything else.

And then are there any laws that are needed for us to do what we want to do as far as protecting this country and our citizens and the economy of this country? Those, if you could do that, because what we would like to do, according to Chairman Royce, is formulate a cybersecurity policy for the United States of America. And we don't want to wait another 20 years. And if you would do that, it would be greatly appreciated. How long do you think it would take? Can we get that in a week, within a week?

Ms. LOTRIONTE. I can give you the legal answers in a day.

Mr. YOHO. Perfect. Thank you.

Mr. BUTLER. A week.

Mr. YOHO. Mr. Chairman, thank you.

Chairman ROYCE. Thank you very much, Mr. Yoho. I appreciate those ideas. And we stand adjourned. And, again, thank you very much, panel.

[Whereupon, at 11:45 a.m., the committee was adjourned.]

APPENDIX

MATERIAL SUBMITTED FOR THE RECORD

FULL COMMITTEE HEARING NOTICE
COMMITTEE ON FOREIGN AFFAIRS
U.S. HOUSE OF REPRESENTATIVES
WASHINGTON, DC 20515-6128

Edward R. Royce (R-CA), Chairman

September 30, 2015

TO: MEMBERS OF THE COMMITTEE ON FOREIGN AFFAIRS

You are respectfully requested to attend an OPEN hearing of the Committee on Foreign Affairs, to be held in Room 2172 of the Rayburn House Office Building (and available live on the Committee website at http://www.ForeignAffairs.house.gov):

DATE: Wednesday, September 30, 2015

TIME: 10:00 a.m.

SUBJECT: Cyber War: Definitions, Deterrence, and Foreign Policy

WITNESSES: James Andrew Lewis, Ph.D.
                 Senior Fellow and Director
                 Strategic Technologies Program
                 Center for Strategic and International Studies

                 Catherine Lotrionte, Ph.D.
                 Director
                 Institute for Law, Science and Global Security
                 Georgetown University

                 Mr. Bob Butler
                 Adjunct Senior Fellow
                 Technology and National Security Program
                 Center for a New American Security

By Direction of the Chairman

The Committee on Foreign Affairs seeks to make its facilities accessible to persons with disabilities. If you are in need of special accommodations, please call 202/225-5021 at least four business days in advance of the event, whenever practicable. Questions with regard to special accommodations in general (including availability of Committee materials in alternative formats and assistive listening devices) may be directed to the Committee.

COMMITTEE ON FOREIGN AFFAIRS
MINUTES OF FULL COMMITTEE HEARING

Day __Wednesday__ Date _____ 9/30/2015 _____ Room _____ 2172 _____

Starting Time _____ 10:11 _____ Ending Time _____ 11:45 _____

Recesses ___ 0 ___ (___ to ___) (___ to ___) (___ to ___) (___ to ___) (___ to ___) (___ to ___)

Presiding Member(s)

Chairman Edward R. Royce, Rep. Matt Salmon

Check all of the following that apply:

Open Session ☑   Electronically Recorded (taped) ☑
Executive (closed) Session ☐   Stenographic Record ☑
Televised ☑

TITLE OF HEARING:

Cyber War: Definitions, Deterrence, and Foreign Policy

COMMITTEE MEMBERS PRESENT:

See attached.

NON-COMMITTEE MEMBERS PRESENT:

none

HEARING WITNESSES: Same as meeting notice attached? Yes ☑ No ☐
(If "no", please list below and include title, agency, department, or organization.)

STATEMENTS FOR THE RECORD: *(List any statements submitted for the record.)*

SFR - Rep. Gerald Connolly
QFR - Chairman Edward R. Royce
QFR - Rep. Eliot Engel
QFR - Rep. Dana Rohrabacher
QFR - Rep. Mark Meadows
QFR - Rep. Ted Yoho

TIME SCHEDULED TO RECONVENE _____
or
TIME ADJOURNED *11:45* _____

Jean Marter, Director of Committee Operations

HOUSE COMMITTEE ON FOREIGN AFFAIRS
FULL COMMITTEE HEARING

PRESENT	MEMBER	PRESENT	MEMBER
X	Edward R. Royce, CA	X	Eliot L. Engel, NY
X	Christopher H. Smith, NJ	X	Brad Sherman, CA
	Ileana Ros-Lehtinen, FL		Gregory W. Meeks, NY
X	Dana Rohrabacher, CA	X	Albio Sires, NJ
X	Steve Chabot, OH	X	Gerald E. Connolly, VA
	Joe Wilson, SC		Theodore E. Deutch, FL
	Michael T. McCaul, TX		Brian Higgins, NY
X	Ted Poe, TX	X	Karen Bass, CA
X	Matt Salmon, AZ		William Keating, MA
X	Darrell Issa, CA		David Cicilline, RI
	Tom Marino, PA		Alan Grayson, FL
	Jeff Duncan, SC		Ami Bera, CA
	Mo Brooks, AL	X	Alan S. Lowenthal, CA
	Paul Cook, CA		Grace Meng, NY
X	Randy Weber, TX		Lois Frankel, FL
X	Scott Perry, PA		Tulsi Gabbard, HI
X	Ron DeSantis, FL	X	Joaquin Castro, TX
	Mark Meadows, NC		Robin Kelly, IL
X	Ted Yoho, FL		Brendan Boyle, PA
X	Curt Clawson, FL		
	Scott DesJarlais, TN		
	Reid Ribble, WI		
	Dave Trott, MI		
	Lee Zeldin, NY		
	Dan Donovan, NY		

Statement for the Record
Submitted by Mr. Connolly of Virginia

The internet is ubiquitous. We depend on it for personal health, national security, and innumerable daily tasks. We take its presence for granted and benefit from its convenience. However, we have not fully vetted the role it plays in the institutions and policies that were created without consideration of cyber-enabled activities, many of which predate the invention of the internet.

At the nexus of cyber-related issues and the jurisdiction of the House Foreign Affairs Committee lies a relatively unexplored area of U.S. law and American foreign policy. This Committee must examine the way in which cyber-enabled activities are accounted for in the provisions of U.S. Code that fall within the Committee's jurisdiction. Our findings could have far-reaching implications on activities such as leading international efforts to deter cyber warfare, levying sanctions in response to cyberattacks, and, this Committee's most sacred charge, vetting an Authorization for the Use of Military Force (AUMF).

Multilateral institutions and bilateral alliances alike are wrestling with the ways in which cyber-activities fit into the agreements and expectations that undergird international partnerships. NATO has developed the *Tallinn Manual* to outline how cyber conflict should be treated under international law. Additionally, the United Nations Secretariat recently published a report adopted by the Group Governmental Experts on Developments in the Field of Information and Telecommunications in the Context of International Security. This report attempts to establish a set of norms for States' behavior as related to information and communications technologies (ICT). The report also sets out to define ICT's role in conflict and international law.

In areas where the U.S. cannot reach consensus with our international partners on how to avoid cyber conflict, we have additional tools at our disposal to deter cyber-enabled threats to U.S. national security. In Executive Order 13964, the President deployed the threat of sanctions against individuals overseas who carry out cyber-enabled commercial espionage or attacks on critical infrastructure. The threat of using these sanctions against China is widely credited as helping the U.S. secure commitments from China that it would not sponsor cyber espionage or block investigations conducted by U.S. Computer Emergency Response Teams (CERTs).

To authorize these sanctions, the President declared a national emergency and exercised authorities granted to the Presidency under the International Emergency Economic Powers Act (IEEPA) and the National Emergencies Act (NEA). To demonstrate resolve in Congress on this matter, it may be prudent to grant the President standing authority to administer a robust sanctions regime against individuals who would seek to harm American commercial or security interests.

Should international forums and deterrence fail to prevent an attack on the U.S. or one of our allies, the parameters of an acceptable U.S. cyber-enabled response are not entirely settled and neither is the authorization a President would need to carry out such a response. While a cyber-enabled response may not deploy troops into direct hostilities as they are traditionally defined, such a response should not be immune from Congressional oversight or authorization requirements, especially if it could be defined as cyber armed conflict.

I look forward to hearing from our witnesses today on ways in which the U.S. can supplement its cyber rulemaking activities in international fora with concrete domestic policies that deter cyber threats. This discussion would also benefit from suggestions on how U.S. national security laws must be amended to accommodate cyber-enabled activities. We must put U.S. cyber defense on firm legal ground both at home and abroad.

Center for a
New American
Security

October 19, 2015

Testimony before the House Foreign Affairs Committee
Answers to Take-Back Questions

Robert J. Butler, Adjunct Senior Fellow
Center for a New American Security

Questions for the Record

From Chairman Royce:

- **Dr. Lotrionte and Mr. Butler.** If a cyber attack took down our financial system, or took down the electrical grid, would the United States consider it a use of force? If so, how would we determine who to strike back, and who to strike against?

- **BOB BUTLER RESPONSE:** Yes, a cyber-induced attack on our financial system or our electric grid which resulted in sustained disruption and/or destruction would be considered a use of force and armed aggression against the United States. As I mentioned in my written testimony, a key to assessing responsive action would be our ability to attribute the attack to a particular actor. Attribution is a foundational capability to any deterrence strategy. To attribute, we would be relying on the sensors and analysis of our national security apparatus, industry and other (allied) partners.

Rep. Rohrabacher:

- **Dr. Lewis, Dr. Lotrionte, and Mr. Butler.** We are going to need to know how we can verify that there has been an attack, verify who the attack is from, determine what type of protection that we may have that will nullify or at least protect us against these attacks. What types of systems do we need? What are our options of retaliation? What will justify a type of retaliation?

- **BOB BUTLER RESPONSE:** We need instrumentation across all of our national security and critical infrastructure systems so we can measure attack damage and identify source. In terms of responding and as I stated in my written testimony, we should consider options that extend across all of our instruments of power, including diplomatic, law enforcement, economic/trade, information and military, and develop courses of action appropriately. Attack damage assessment, to include understanding the loss of operational, economic and intelligence value, should be the primary drivers in justifying the scope of our response. The type of response needs to be weighed IAW national and customary international laws of proportionality and reciprocity.

Rep. Yoho:

- **Dr. Lewis, Dr. Lotrionte, and Mr. Butler.** What do we do when another country, a nation state, works through a proxy, maybe Hezbollah or in the future some terrorist organization, but we know it was directed by a nation state?

- **BOB BUTLER RESPSONSE:** Under customary international law, the nation-state shares the same liability as the surrogate, in this case, the terrorist organization. As discussed previously, a key to understanding how to respond is our ability to attribute.

- **Dr. Lewis, Dr. Lotrionte, and Mr. Butler.** What is your recommendation to help facilitate our government working with private industry, or vice versa, industry working with our government, to prevent or alert each other about attacks? Are there any laws prohibiting us in follow through, on these? Is something prohibiting us?

- **BOB BUTLER RESPONSE:** As I discussed in my written and oral testimonies, we should be focused on enabling not only information sharing, but joint solutioning among US government entities, industry and other partners. Joint solutioning could include everything from shared indications and warning to certified active defense. To achieve this objective, we need to provide liability protection and other incentives to build effective public-private sector partnerships. Laws may need to be updated, starting with the Critical Infrastructure Partnership Advisory Council (CIPAC) statute.

- **Dr. Lewis, Dr. Lotrionte, and Mr. Butler.** Are there any laws that are needed for us to do what we want to do in as far as protecting this country, our citizens, and the economy of this country?

- **BOB BUTLER RESPONSE:** Besides the CIPAC statute, the Defense Production Act, the Safety Act, the Electronic Communications Privacy Act, the Computer Fraud and Abuse Act, the Digital Millennium Copyright Act and other system/economic protection statutes should all be reviewed and updated.

Georgetown University
School of Foreign Service

October 29, 2015

Testimony before the House Foreign Affairs Committee
Answers to Take-Back Questions

Catherine Lotrionte, Georgetown University

Questions for the Record

From Chairman Royce:

- **Dr. Lotrionte.** Which U.S. government agencies are responsible for addressing cyber war related threats and response and recovery efforts? Should the Department of Defense protect the cyber security of the U.S. homeland from significant cyber attacks? Is it time to look at standing up another branch of the military, as the Air Force was stood up during the Second World War?

- **CATHERINE LOTRIONTE RESPONSE:** The Department of Defense is responsible for addressing cyber conflict issues including using force (cyber or kinetic) in defense of the U.S. in response to attacks against the U.S. or U.S. entities abroad whether those attacks against the U.S. were by cyber or kinetic means. The U.S. President would decide under what circumstances the Department of Defense, specifically Cyber Command, would be authorized to take action that would constitute uses of force under international law. The intelligence community has a role in collecting and analyzing any information about future threats against the U.S. in cyberspace. The civilian agencies such DHS and FEMA have a role in assisting with any recovery measures after an attack. FBI would be responsible for investigating after any attack against the U.S., supporting the intelligence community in its intelligence role in assessing the threats prior to an attack, and assisting the victim companies after an attack. I do believe that it is time to study the prospect of establishing a separate Cyber Force within the Department of Defense. In addition, to support the domestic efforts related to recovery, there should be consideration of the value of establishing a civilian "Cyber Corps" similar to the Peace Corps, but with a focus on domestic assistance.

- **Dr. Lotrionte and Mr. Butler.** If a cyber attack took down our financial system, or took down the electrical grid, would the United States consider it a use of force? If so, how would we determine who to strike back, and who to strike against?

- **CATHERINE LOTRIONTE RESPONSE**: Yes, assuming that a cyber operation against the U.S. financial system or electrical grid resulted in a sustained and extensive disruption of the systems, resulting in a prolonged disruption or even destruction of those systems, such a cyber operation could constitute a use of force under a legal analysis. It would then be up to the President and Congress to determine how the U.S. would respond to the actions. Attribution would be critical in contemplating a response and depending on the level of certainty on attribution U.S. government responsive actions may vary (ranging from diplomatic actions, law enforcement actions or military actions). If the U.S. were to determine that a lethal use of force in response was appropriate there would likely need to be a high level of certainty about who was responsible for the attack and if the attack was carried out by non-state actors those actions would need to be attributed to a state actor in order to hold a state responsible for those attacks. In order to maximize the ability to attribute such attacks it would be important to work with the private sector, along with the intelligence community and even international partners. Furthermore, although the U.S. would not need to justify the use of force in self-defense to any court or the UN Security Council (UNSC) prior to taking actions against such a continuing threat, the U.S. will likely need to be prepared to defend its actions after the fact. Therefore, the U.S. government ought to consider what information it would be willing or able to discuss among partners, at an international court, the UNSC or other international fora. Such information would provide the basis for attribution, some of which may need to be disclosed to justify U.S. responsive actions.

From Ranking Member Engel:
- **Dr. Lotrionte.** As the United States works to develop global norms in customary international law governing cyber conflict, what legal clarifications are needed to ensure that we are able to prevent and respond to cyber threats by terrorist groups and other non-state actors?

CATHERINE LOTRIONTE RESPONSE:
- The 2015 report by the UN Group of Governmental Experts (GGE) on "Developments in the Field of Information and Telecommunications in the context of International Security" included a provision that supported the principle of state responsibility under international law for cyberspace in stating that states are responsible for ensuring that their territory is not used by individuals to carry out harmful actions outside of their territory against others. The UN GGE was composed of 20 states including Russia, China, and the United States. While explicitly getting agreement that this legal principle applies in cyberspace was significant, it is necessary to bring more clarity to what this means exactly. For example, there is currently no agreement as to what level of due diligence the state must take to prevent and/or stop cyber attacks emanating from the state's territory. Nor is there any agreement on what the victim state can do under the circumstances that such an attack occurs from the territory of another state. One option is to identify the specific actions that are expected from the state once the victim state notifies that state of the attack. In the context of kinetic terrorists attacks, stemming from the

attacks on 9/11, the U.S. accepted an "unwilling or unable" test in assessing whether the state from which the attack emanated would be held responsible for the attacks. This may be a useful test to apply in the context of cyber attacks as well.

From Rep. Rohrabacher:
- **Dr. Lewis, Dr. Lotrionte, and Mr. Butler.** We are going to need to know how we can verify that there has been an attack, verify who the attack is from, determine what type of protection that we may have that will nullify or at least protect us against these attacks. What types of systems do we need? What are our options of retaliation? What will justify a type of retaliation?
- **CATHERINE LOTRIONTE RESPONSE:** In terms of systems that would provide the government with the necessary information related to level of damage and attribution of the attacker, the government will need to have a broad understanding of what is happening on the systems across the country to include the private sector critical infrastructure and other private businesses. Getting this information will require the government to work cooperatively with the private sector so they can share that information about what they are seeing on their networks with the government agencies. As I mentioned previously in the above answers, the options for the U.S. in response to any cyber attacks will depend upon the resulting effects of the attack and whether such actions were equivalent to physical effects from an adversary. Any such U.S. responsive actions should comply with both U.S. and international law. The U.S. has publicly stated numerous times that it will operate under the principles of international law related to the recourse to the use of force in self-defense which means that any U.S. responsive action would need to be both "necessary" (the only way to resolve the threat) and "proportionate" to the threat.

From Rep. Yoho:
- **Dr. Lewis, Dr. Lotrionte, and Mr. Butler.** What do we do when another country, a nation state, works through a proxy, maybe Hezbollah or in the future some terrorist organization, but we know it was directed by a nation state?
- **CATHERINE LOTRIONTE RESPONSE:** As I mentioned above in the answers related to attribution, under international law, in order to hold another nation responsible for such terrorist non-state actors' actions, the U.S. would need to attribute those actions to the state. Depending upon ones interpretation of current international law related to thresholds for attribution the U.S. would need to know either that that state has "effective control" over those proxies (Nicaragua case) or "overall control" over them (Tadic case). Again, although the U.S. would have the legal authority to use force in self-defense after an attack or in the face of an imminent attack without getting prior approval for such action in self-defense, it will likely need to be prepared to justify its actions after the fact either before a court like the International Court of Justice or the UNSC or to allies and other states.
- **Dr. Lewis, Dr. Lotrionte, and Mr. Butler.** What is your recommendation to help facilitate our government working with private industry, or vice versa, industry working with our government, to prevent or alert each other about attacks? Are

there any laws prohibiting us in follow through, on these? IS something prohibiting us?

- **CATHERINE LOTRIONTE RESPONSE**: There needs to be a very robust and efficient, if not automated, format for the private sector and the government to quickly share timely threat information that they each have access to. Going beyond just sharing the known signatures there needs to be awareness of the newest threats and other indicators of incoming attacks both from the private sector as they see the threats and the government. This may have to include understanding of vulnerabilities or zero day exploits that the government may otherwise may want to retain only in the government. In order for the private sector to freely share the information it has with the government there is a need for legislation that would provide some form of liability protection for the companies. In addition to sharing indicators and warnings, the private sector could be supporting the defensive work of the government, in partnership with the government, by actively taking part in a form of "active defense." Such action by the private sector ought to be under the oversight of the government whether through a contract relationship or certification process that ensures transparency and oversight to the government as well as liability protections for the companies as long as they operate within the scope of the defined terms of the relationship.

- **Dr. Lewis, Dr. Lotrionte, and Mr. Butler**. Are there any laws that are needed for us to do what we want to do in as far as protecting this country, our citizens, and the economy of this country?

- **CATHERINE LOTRIONTE RESPONSE**: First, all privacy laws should be reviewed in order to determine if there are any needed amendments to the laws in order for effective information sharing between the private sector and the government. Second, the regulatory authorities of certain entities such as the SEC, FTC, FCC should be reviewed in order to determine if these entities need any further authorities in order to impose improved cyber security in the private sector industry, particularly in the critical infrastructure sectors. Third, Congress ought to review amending the War Powers Resolution if there is a desire for the expected reporting and consultation from the President when/if conducting cyber operations abroad. As it is currently written such cyber operations would not be covered by the statute. Fourth, as far as having the private sector support the government in partner in defense, active defense, the Computer Fraud and Abuse Act (CFAA) would likely need to be amended in order to clarify what acts specifically would not be criminalized under CFAA. As far as international law is concerned, the US has the authority to act in response to any threat under traditional international law. Those some laws (UN Charter, customary international law, Laws of Armed Conflict) would apply in cyberspace. The questions that are still not resolved is the thresholds for acting in self-defense and what specific acts would be lawful in self-defense. In other words, when would an adversary's act rise to the level of an armed attack in cyberspace such that the US could act in self-defense under Article 51 of the UN Charter. And what is a "necessary and proportionate" response in self-defense in cyberspace? I discussed this more in my written statement for the record.

Congressman Mark Meadows (NC-11)
Full Foreign Affairs Committee Hearing
"Cyber War: Definitions, Deterrence, and Foreign Policy"
Wednesday, September 30, 2015, 10:00 am

Question 1:

The text of the agreement reads: "Neither country's government will conduct or knowingly support cyber-enabled theft of intellectual property". During his visit, President Xi told the Wall Street Journal that China does not currently engage in economic espionage. He said: "China takes cybersecurity very seriously. China is also a victim of hacking. The Chinese government does not engage in theft of commercial secrets in any form, nor does it encourage or support Chinese companies to engage in such practices in any way."

Mr. Lewis, you state that China alone is responsible for more than half of all economic espionage in the United States. Given the agreement and President Xi's statement, what has China really agreed to? To not engage in behavior that they already deny engaging in? Thus, does China actually have to change its behavior?

Question 2:

Following President Xi's visit to Washington, President Obama also spoke of "architecture to govern behavior in cyberspace that is enforceable and clear". One aspect of the agreement is to cooperate on matters combatting cybercrime. The United States and China have different definitions of cybercrime

By coming to an agreement with China, have we agreed to their definition?

Question 3:

Mr. Lewis, you state in your testimony that there can be no cybersecurity without international agreement on state behavior. The Obama administration has been pushing for international norm development in cybersecurity. China has an entirely different view of the internet, cyber war, and cyber espionage. Most importantly, China views the internet as a threat to their control of the population. They have also used the internet as a threat abroad. Is it possible to come to an agreement and develop norms with China when we come from completely different places in terms of how we view the internet, warfare, and cyberspace in general? Bad actors, such as Russia and China have no real incentive to agree with us on these norms – so what do we expect? Can we come to a common agreement? Even if we do, will they behave any differently?

Question 4:

Language in the agreement indicates that Obama views China as a partner, affirming China's claim that it is a "fellow victim" of cybercrime. This is a problem and a rhetorical shift.

Does this indicate that President Obama sees China as a partner and not a perpetrator?

Mr. Lewis, you note in your testimony that China is responsible for more than half of all cybercrime in the U.S. Why is the Obama Administration treating the Chinese as moral equals on this matter, when we all know they are the primary perpetrators?

[NOTE: No responses were received by the committee to the above questions prior to printing.]

www.ingramcontent.com/pod-product-compliance
Lightning Source LLC
Chambersburg PA
CBHW081240280526

45787CB00006B/2745